GOD Loves HER

40-Day Devotional Journal

God Loves Her 40-Day Devotional Journal

The devotional readings collected in this book were previously published over a span of years in *Our Daily Bread* devotional booklets that are distributed around the world in more than fifty languages.

Interior design by Michael J. Williams

ISBN: 978-1-64070-451-0

Printed in the United States of America
26 27 28 29 30 31 32 33 / 8 7 6 5 4 3 2 1

HOW TO USE THIS BOOK

The women writers of *Our Daily Bread* welcome you on a refreshing forty-day journey with the One who loves you unconditionally and understands you completely.

You're invited to

Draw closer to God through forty beautiful devotions on God's nearness,

Meditate on Scripture with curated Bible passages and reflection questions—to let your heart ponder truth and life,

Pray and journal using prompts that free you to love God with your heart, mind, and emotions.

Let these forty days lead you to lift your eyes to the One who sees you with gentleness, who loves you without conditions or limits, and who desires to refresh your soul with His perfect peace.

> The eternal God is your refuge, and underneath are the everlasting arms.
>
> Deuteronomy 33:27

Anna Haggard
General Editor

DAY 1

PSALM 136:1–9 NLT

Give thanks to the Lord, for he is good!
His faithful love endures forever.
Give thanks to the God of gods.
His faithful love endures forever.
Give thanks to the Lord of lords.
His faithful love endures forever.

Give thanks to him who alone does mighty miracles.
His faithful love endures forever.
Give thanks to him who made the heavens so skillfully.
His faithful love endures forever.
Give thanks to him who placed the earth among the waters.
His faithful love endures forever.
Give thanks to him who made the heavenly lights—
His faithful love endures forever.
the sun to rule the day,
His faithful love endures forever.
and the moon and stars to rule the night.
His faithful love endures forever.

The almighty God who sustains the universe has chosen to love me freely and unconditionally.

FOREVER LOVE

Years ago, my four-year-old son gave me a framed wooden heart mounted on a metal plate with the word forever painted in its center. "I love you forever, Mommy," he said.

I thanked him with a hug. "I love you more."

That priceless gift still assures me of my son's never-ending love. On tough days, God uses that sweet present to comfort and encourage me as He affirms I'm deeply loved.

The frame also reminds me of the gift of God's everlasting love, as expressed throughout His Word and confirmed by His Spirit. We can trust God's unchanging goodness and sing grateful praises that confirm His enduring love, as the psalmist does (Psalm 136:1). We can exalt the Lord as greater than and above all (vv. 2–3), as we reflect on His endless wonders and unlimited understanding (vv. 4–5). The God who loves us forever is the conscious and caring Maker of the heavens and earth, who maintains control of time itself (vv. 6–9).

We can rejoice because the everlasting love the psalmist sang about is the same continuing love our all-powerful Creator and Sustainer pours into the lives of His children today. No matter what we're facing, the One who made us and remains with us strengthens us by asserting He loves us unconditionally and completely.

Xochitl Dixon

Write

As you begin this forty-day journey, reflect on your personal relationship with God. How would you like to draw closer to Jesus in the days ahead?

We know and rely on the love God has for us. God is love.

1 JOHN 4:16

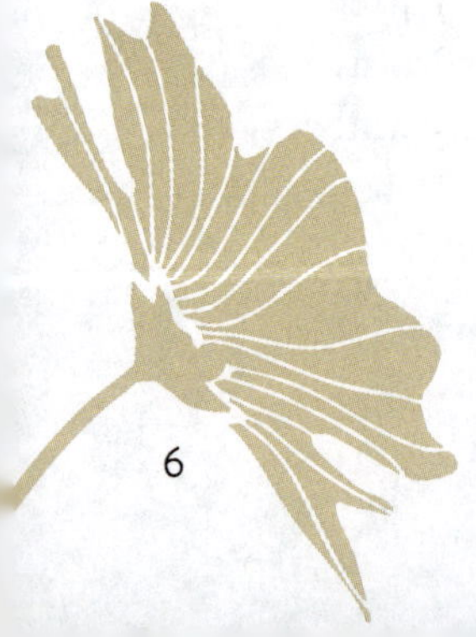

Connect

The Hebrew word *hesed* shows up twenty-six times in Psalm 136—a rich Hebrew word translated as "faithful love" in the New International Version. But *hesed* is loaded with more meaning than any one English word can communicate. It's a love without limits—unearned yet freely given, never-ending, completely committed.

Check out just a few ways Bible translations share about this love.

His steadfast love endures forever. (ESV)

His love never quits. Thank the God of all gods, *His love never quits.* Thank the Lord of all lords. *His love never quits.* (MSG)

His mercy endures forever. (NKJV)

His loving-kindness lasts forever. (NLV)

His faithfulness is everlasting. (NASB)

Sit with one translation that speaks to your heart and journal why it's meaningful to you.

Invite God to reveal His infinite love to you in new, fresh ways over the next forty days.

DAY 2

PROVERBS 19:20–23

Listen to advice and accept discipline,
and at the end you will be counted among the wise.

Many are the plans in a person's heart,
but it is the LORD's purpose that prevails.

What a person desires is unfailing love;
better to be poor than a liar.

The fear of the LORD leads to life;
then one rests content, untouched by trouble.

God's plans for my future are always good, purposeful, and filled with hope.

IMPERFECT PLANS

I was exploring a library on the bottom floor of a new community center when an overhead crash suddenly shook the room. A few minutes later it happened again, and then again. An agitated librarian finally explained that a weight-lifting area was positioned directly above the library, and the noise occurred every time someone dropped a weight. Architects and designers had carefully planned many aspects of this state-of-the-art facility, yet someone had forgotten to locate the library away from all the action.

In life as well, our plans are often flawed. We overlook important considerations. And it's tough to account for accidents or surprises as we make plans. Although planning helps us avoid financial shortfalls, time crunches, and health issues, even the most thorough strategies can't eliminate all problems from our lives. We live in a post-Eden, imperfect world.

With God's help, we can find the balance between prudently considering the future (Proverbs 6:6–8) and responding to difficulties. God often has a purpose for the trouble He allows into our lives. He may use it to develop patience in us, to increase our faith, or simply to bring us closer to Him. The Bible reminds us, "Many are the plans in a person's heart, but it is the LORD's purpose that prevails" (Proverbs 19:21). As we submit our goals and hopes for the future to Jesus, He'll show us what He wants to accomplish in us and through us—no matter what the circumstances.

Jennifer Benson Schuldt

Pray

Bring to Jesus an unfulfilled dream or desire.

Connect

With Jesus, take inventory of what matters most to you right now—your priorities, goals, and plans. As you share them with God, listen for the Holy Spirit's guidance about what to take hold of, what to adjust, and what to let go of.

Write

Think back to a time when your plans or expectations weren't met and talk honestly about it with Jesus.

Many are the plans in a person's heart, but it is the Lord's purpose that prevails.

PROVERBS 19:21

DAY 3

PSALM 139:1–6, 23–24 NLT

O LORD, you have examined my heart
  and know everything about me.
You know when I sit down or stand up.
  You know my thoughts even when I'm far away.
You see me when I travel
  and when I rest at home.
  You know everything I do.
You know what I am going to say
  even before I say it, LORD.
You go before me and follow me.
  You place your hand of blessing on my head.
Such knowledge is too wonderful for me,
  too great for me to understand! . . .

Search me, O God, and know my heart;
  test me and know my anxious thoughts.
Point out anything in me that offends you,
  and lead me along the path of everlasting life.

I am completely known and fully loved.

GOD KNOWS YOUR STORY

As I drove home after lunch with my best friend, I thanked God out loud for her. She knows me and loves me in spite of things I don't love about myself. She's one of a small circle of people who accept me as I am—my quirks, habits, and screw-ups. Still, there are parts of my story I resist sharing even with her and others that I love—times where I've clearly not been the hero, times I've been judgmental or unkind or unloving.

But God does know my whole story. He's the One I can freely talk to even if I'm reluctant to talk with others.

The familiar words of Psalm 139 describe the intimacy we enjoy with our Sovereign King. He knows us completely (v. 1). He's "familiar with all [our] ways" (v. 3). He invites us to come to Him with our confusion, our anxious thoughts, and our struggles with temptation. When we're willing to yield completely to Him, He reaches out to restore and rewrite the parts of our story that make us sad because we've wandered from Him.

God knows us better than anyone else ever can, and still He loves us! When we daily surrender ourselves to Him and seek to know Him more fully, He can change our story for His glory. He's the Author who's continuing to write it.

Cindy Hess Kasper

Search me, O God, and know my heart; test me and know my anxious thoughts.

PSALM 139:23 NLT

Write

How has God restored and redemptively rewritten your story? Let gratitude to God wash over you for this amazing gift of grace.

Connect

Scripture is like a feast for your soul. Choose a word or phrase from Psalm 139 to slowly savor and allow it to nourish you. Ask Jesus how He may be using it to quietly reassure and encourage you today.

Pray

Where are you struggling with temptation or shame? Share your burden with the One who knows your whole story.

ISAIAH 49:14–18, 22–23 ESV

But Zion said, "The Lord has forsaken me;
my Lord has forgotten me."

"Can a woman forget her nursing child,
that she should have no compassion on the son of her
womb?
Even these may forget,
yet I will not forget you.
Behold, I have engraved you on the palms of my hands;
your walls are continually before me.
Your builders make haste;
your destroyers and those who laid you waste go out
from you.
Lift up your eyes around and see;
they all gather, they come to you.
As I live, declares the Lord,
you shall put them all on as an ornament;
you shall bind them on as a bride does. . . .

Thus says the Lord God:
"Behold, I will lift up my hand to the nations,
and raise my signal to the peoples;
and they shall bring your sons in their arms,
and your daughters shall be carried on their shoulders.
Kings shall be your foster fathers,
and their queens your nursing mothers.
With their faces to the ground they shall bow down to you,
and lick the dust of your feet.
Then you will know that I am the Lord;
those who wait for me shall not be put to shame."

Nothing escapes God's notice or is outside His attentive care.

ENGRAVED ON GOD'S HANDS

It makes no logical sense, but when my parents died within a three-month period, I feared they would forget me. Of course, they were no longer on earth, but that left me with a large uncertainty. I was a young, unmarried adult and wondered how to navigate life without them. Feeling really single and alone, I sought God.

One morning I told Him about my irrational fear and the sadness it brought (even though He knew it already). The Scripture passage that came for the devotional I read that day was Isaiah 49: "Can a woman forget her nursing child . . . ? Even these may forget, yet I will not forget you" (v. 15 ESV). God reassured His people through Isaiah that He had not forgotten them and later promised to restore them to Himself through sending His Son Jesus. But the words ministered to my heart too. It's rare for a mother or a father to forget their child, yet it's possible. But God? No way. "I have engraved you on the palms of my hands" (v. 16), He said.

God's answer to me could have brought more fear. But the peace He gave because of His own remembrance of me was exactly what I needed. It was the start of discovering that God is even closer than a parent or anyone else, and He knows the way to help us with everything—even our fears.

Anne Cetas

Connect

Isaiah 49 is filled with beautiful images that speak to God's endless love. Circle or underline an image that grabs your attention or provides you with a sense of comfort or deep peace. Why is it meaningful to you?

Pray

What worries or concerns you today? Honestly share your anxiety with Jesus. He welcomes your coming to Him vulnerably and openly!

Write

When have you felt overlooked or forgotten by others or by God, and what thoughts and feelings come up as you think about that experience? Bring your memory, and your thoughts and feelings about it, to God in prayer.

I will not forget you.

ISAIAH 49:15 ESV

HABAKKUK 3:6, 16–19

He stood, and shook the earth;
he looked, and made the nations tremble.
The ancient mountains crumbled
and the age-old hills collapsed—
but he marches on forever. . . .

I heard and my heart pounded,
my lips quivered at the sound;
decay crept into my bones,
and my legs trembled.
Yet I will wait patiently for the day of calamity
to come on the nation invading us.
Though the fig tree does not bud
and there are no grapes on the vines,
though the olive crop fails
and the fields produce no food,
though there are no sheep in the pen
and no cattle in the stalls,
yet I will rejoice in the Lord,
I will be joyful in God my Savior.

The Sovereign Lord is my strength;
he makes my feet like the feet of a deer,
he enables me to tread on the heights.

Trusting in who God is unleashes true joy.

FINDING JOY IN PRAISE

When the famous British writer C. S. Lewis first gave his life to Jesus, he initially resisted praising God. In fact, he called it "a stumbling block." His struggle was "in the suggestion that God Himself demanded it." Yet Lewis finally realized "it is in the process of being worshipped that God communicates His presence" to His people. Then we, "in perfect love with God," find joy in Him no more separable "than the brightness a mirror receives" from the "brightness it sheds."

The prophet Habakkuk arrived at this conclusion centuries earlier. After complaining to God about evils aimed at the people of Judah, Habakkuk came to see that praising Him leads to joy—in trusting in who He is. Thus, even in a national or world crisis, God is still great. As the prophet declared: "Though the fig tree does not bud and there are no grapes on the vines, though the olive crop fails and the fields produce no food, though there are no sheep in the pen and no cattle in the stalls, yet I will rejoice in the Lord" (Habakkuk 3:17–18). "I will be joyful in God my Savior," he added.

As C. S. Lewis realized, "The whole world rings with praise." Habakkuk, likewise, surrendered to praising God always, finding rich joy in the One who "marches on forever" (v. 6).

Patricia Raybon

Write

Think back to a time of worship where God made His presence known to you. What was it like to personally meet with God, and how does it feel knowing that God wanted to connect with you?

Yet I will rejoice in the LORD.

HABAKKUK 3:18

Connect

What is a heartache or trial you are facing? Consider following Habakkuk's example by committing to praise God in the midst of this painful circumstance.

Reflect on God's goodness and identify and name three reasons you can praise Him.

SONG OF SONGS 8:5–7 ESV

Who is that coming up from the wilderness,
leaning on her beloved?

Under the apple tree I awakened you.
There your mother was in labor with you;
there she who bore you was in labor.

Set me as a seal upon your heart,
as a seal upon your arm,
for love is strong as death,
jealousy is fierce as the grave.
Its flashes are flashes of fire,
the very flame of the LORD.
Many waters cannot quench love,
neither can floods drown it.
If a man offered for love
all the wealth of his house,
he would be utterly despised.

God's love is safe and steadfast.

LOVE LOCKS

I stood amazed at the hundreds of thousands of padlocks, many engraved with the initials of sweethearts, attached to every imaginable part of the Pont des Arts bridge in Paris. The pedestrian bridge across the Seine River was inundated with these symbols of love, a couple's declaration of "forever" commitment. In 2014, the love locks were estimated to weigh a staggering fifty tons and had even caused a portion of the bridge to collapse, necessitating the locks' removal.

The presence of so many love locks points to the deep longing we have as human beings for assurance that love is secure. In Song of Songs, an Old Testament book that depicts a dialogue between two lovers, the woman expresses her desire for secure love by asking her beloved to "place me like a seal over your heart, like a seal on your arm" (Song of Songs 8:6). Her longing was to be as safe and secure in his love as a seal impressed on his heart or a ring on his finger.

The longing for enduring romantic love expressed in Song of Songs points us to the New Testament truth in Ephesians that we are marked with the "seal" of God's Spirit (1:13). While human love can be fickle, and locks can be removed from a bridge, Christ's Spirit living in us is a permanent seal demonstrating God's never-ending, committed love for each of His children.

Lisa M. Samra

Set me as a seal upon your heart,
as a seal upon your arm.

SONG OF SONGS 8:6 ESV

Write

Marked with the "seal" of the Holy Spirit, we can rest safely in our relationship with God. Check out how *The Message* captures this reassuring truth:

> It's in Christ that you, once you heard the truth and believed it (this Message of your salvation), found yourselves home free—signed, sealed, and delivered by the Holy Spirit. This down payment from God is the first installment on what's coming, a reminder that we'll get everything God has planned for us, a praising and glorious life. (Ephesians 1:13–14)

What about this amazing promise comforts and encourages you?

Connect

What word or phrase from Song of Songs 8:5–7, today's Bible reading, captures your attention? Why?

Pray

When did you feel close to your beloved Jesus today, and when did you feel distant from Him? Talk with Jesus about it, with the assurance that God desires to draw close to you in love.

DAY 7

ROMANS 8:26–30

In the same way, the Spirit helps us in our weakness. We do not know what we ought to pray for, but the Spirit himself intercedes for us through wordless groans. And he who searches our hearts knows the mind of the Spirit, because the Spirit intercedes for God's people in accordance with the will of God.

And we know that in all things God works for the good of those who love him, who have been called according to his purpose. For those God foreknew he also predestined to be conformed to the image of his Son, that he might be the firstborn among many brothers and sisters. And those he predestined, he also called; those he called, he also justified; those he justified, he also glorified.

Jesus is constantly praying for me.

NO MISUNDERSTANDING

Alexa, Siri, and other voice assistants embedded in smart devices in our homes occasionally misunderstand what we're saying. A six-year-old talked to her family's new device about cookies and a dollhouse. Later her mom received an email saying that an order of seven pounds of cookies and a $170 dollhouse were on their way to her home. Even a talking parrot in London, whose owner had never bought anything online, somehow ordered a package of golden gift boxes without her knowledge. One person asked their device to "turn on the living room lights," and it replied, "There is no pudding room."

There's no such misunderstanding on God's part when we talk with Him. He's never confused, because He knows our hearts better than we do. The Spirit both searches our hearts and understands God's will. The apostle Paul told the churches in Rome that God promises He'll accomplish His good purpose of maturing us and making us more like His Son (Romans 8:28–29). Even when because of "our weakness" we don't know what we need in order to grow, the Spirit prays according to God's will for us (vv. 26–27).

Troubled about how to express yourself to God? Not understanding what or how to pray? Say what you can from the heart. The Spirit will understand and accomplish God's purpose.

Anne Cetas

Pray

Talk with Jesus about whatever is on your heart and mind, no matter how big or small, trusting the Spirit is praying for you and is with you.

Connect

What are you carrying today that feels out of control? Picture handing this circumstance into God's loving, all-powerful arms. What comes to mind as you release this burden to the all-seeing, all-loving Savior?

Write

In your journey of faith, how have you seen God lovingly teaching you and gently encouraging you to grow and become more like Jesus (Romans 8:28–29)?

We know that in all things God works for the good of those who love him.

ROMANS 8:28

DAY 8

JOHN 14:15–18, 26–27

If you love me, keep my commands. And I will ask the Father, and he will give you another advocate to help you and be with you forever—the Spirit of truth. The world cannot accept him, because it neither sees him nor knows him. But you know him, for he lives with you and will be in you. I will not leave you as orphans; I will come to you. . . .

But the Advocate, the Holy Spirit, whom the Father will send in my name, will teach you all things and will remind you of everything I have said to you. Peace I leave with you; my peace I give you. I do not give to you as the world gives. Do not let your hearts be troubled and do not be afraid.

I am never alone. At all times, the Holy Spirit is within me and with me.

NEVER ALONE

While writing a Bible guide for pastors in Indonesia, a writer friend grew fascinated with that nation's culture of togetherness. Called *gotong royong*—meaning "mutual assistance"—the concept is practiced in villages, where neighbors may work together to repair someone's roof or rebuild a bridge or path. In cities too my friend said, "People always go places with someone else—to a doctor's appointment, for example. It's the cultural norm. So you're never alone."

Worldwide, believers in Jesus rejoice in knowing we also are never alone. Our constant and forever companion is the Holy Spirit, the third person of the Trinity. Far more than a loyal friend, the Spirit of God is given to every follower of Christ by our heavenly Father to "help you and be with you forever" (John 14:16).

Jesus promised God's Spirit would come after His own time on earth ended. "I will not leave you as orphans," Jesus said (v. 18). Instead, the Holy Spirit—"the Spirit of truth" who "lives with you and will be in you"—indwells each person who receives Christ as Savior (v. 17).

The Holy Spirit is our Helper, Comforter, Encourager, and Counselor—a constant companion in a world where loneliness can afflict even connected people. May we forever abide in His comforting love and help.

Patricia Raybon

Connect

In your imagination, can you return to a moment where you felt alone? Imagine the scene: the who, what, when, where, and why. As you look around in your memory, ask Jesus to show you where He was present with you.

Pray

God displays His love and care in and through your ordinary and significant moments. Today take special notice of God's activity and, at the end of the day, praise Him for His faithfulness and care.

Write

Which role of the Holy Spirit—as Helper, Comforter, Encourager, or Counselor—have you experienced personally in your walk with God? What was it like for you to sense the Holy Spirit's care?

He will give you another advocate to help you and be with you forever—the Spirit of truth.

JOHN 14:16–17

2 CORINTHIANS 1:3–7 ESV

Blessed be the God and Father of our Lord Jesus Christ, the Father of mercies and God of all comfort, who comforts us in all our affliction, so that we may be able to comfort those who are in any affliction, with the comfort with which we ourselves are comforted by God. For as we share abundantly in Christ's sufferings, so through Christ we share abundantly in comfort too. If we are afflicted, it is for your comfort and salvation; and if we are comforted, it is for your comfort, which you experience when you patiently endure the same sufferings that we suffer. Our hope for you is unshaken, for we know that as you share in our sufferings, you will also share in our comfort.

God comforts me in my struggles, enabling me to offer His care to others.

THE GOD OF ALL COMFORT

Radamenes was just a kitten when his owner dropped him off at an animal shelter, thinking he was too ill to recover. The kitten was nursed back to health and adopted by the vet. He then became a full-time resident at the shelter and now spends his days "comforting" cats and dogs—just out of surgery or recovering from an illness—through his warm presence and gentle purr.

That story is a small picture of what our loving God does for us—and what we can do for others in return. He cares for us in our sickness and struggles, and He soothes us with His presence. The apostle Paul in 2 Corinthians calls our God "the Father of mercies and God of all comfort" (1:3 ESV). When we are discouraged, depressed, or mistreated, He's there for us. When we turn to Him in prayer, He "comforts us in all our affliction" (v. 4 ESV).

But verse 4 doesn't end there. Paul, who had experienced intense suffering, continues, "so that we may be able to comfort those who are in any affliction, with the comfort with which we ourselves are comforted by God" (ESV). Our Father comforts us, and when we've experienced His comfort, we're enabled to comfort others.

Our compassionate Savior, who suffered for us, is more than able to comfort us in our suffering and distress (v. 5). He helps us through our pain and equips us to do the same for others.

Alyson Kieda

[God] comforts us in all our affliction, so that we may be able to comfort those who are in any affliction, with the comfort with which we ourselves are comforted by God.

2 CORINTHIANS 1:3 ESV

Write

In seasons of heartache and hurt, how has God comforted and encouraged you? How have you comforted and encouraged someone else?

Connect

Is there someone you could encourage, support, or simply reach out to this week? What steps could you take to make this happen?

Pray

Where in your life do you long to feel God's comforting presence right now? Invite your gentle Savior to meet you right there.

DAY 10

1 JOHN 4:7–19 NLT

Dear friends, let us continue to love one another, for love comes from God. Anyone who loves is a child of God and knows God. But anyone who does not love does not know God, for God is love.

God showed how much he loved us by sending his one and only Son into the world so that we might have eternal life through him. This is real love—not that we loved God, but that he loved us and sent his Son as a sacrifice to take away our sins.

Dear friends, since God loved us that much, we surely ought to love each other. No one has ever seen God. But if we love each other, God lives in us, and his love is brought to full expression in us.

And God has given us his Spirit as proof that we live in him and he in us. Furthermore, we have seen with our own eyes and now testify that the Father sent his Son to be the Savior of the world. All who declare that Jesus is the Son of God have God living in them, and they live in God. We know how much God loves us, and we have put our trust in his love.

God is love, and all who live in love live in God, and God lives in them. And as we live in God, our love grows more perfect. So we will not be afraid on the day of judgment, but we can face him with confidence because we live like Jesus here in this world.

Such love has no fear, because perfect love expels all fear. If we are afraid, it is for fear of punishment, and this shows that we have not fully experienced his perfect love. We love each other because he loved us first.

I'm forever held in God's limitless love and grace.

"LOVE YOU—WHOLE WORLD"

My three-year old niece, Jenna, has an expression that never fails to melt my heart. When she loves something (really loves it), be it banana cream pie, jumping on the trampoline, or playing Frisbee, she'll proclaim, "I love it—whole world!" ("whole world" accompanied with a dramatic sweep of her arms).

Sometimes I wonder, When's the last time I've dared to love like that? With nothing held back, completely unafraid?

"God is love," John wrote, repeatedly (1 John 4:8, 16), perhaps because the truth that God's love—not our anger, fear, or shame—is the deepest foundation of reality, is hard for us grown-ups to "get." The world divides us into camps based on what we're most afraid of—and all too often we join in, ignoring or villainizing the voices that challenge our preferred vision of reality.

Yet amid the deception and power struggles (vv. 5–6), the truth of God's love remains, a light that shines in the darkness, inviting us to learn the path of humility, trust, and love (1:7–9; 3:18). For no matter what painful truths the light uncovers, we can know that we'll still be loved (4:10, 18; Romans 8:1).

When Jenna leans over and whispers to me, "I love you—whole world!" I whisper back, "I love you—whole world!" And I'm grateful for a gentle reminder that every moment I'm held in limitless love and grace.

Monica La Rose

Pray

Is there anything that causes you to doubt God's faithful love for you? Take a few moments to invite Jesus to meet you in that fear.

Connect

Imagine yourself held in the arms of your heavenly Father. How does it feel to be lovingly held by God?

Write

In 1 John 4, we read that "God is love . . . perfect love expels all fear" (vv. 16, 18 NLT). Sit with that beautiful truth and let it reassure and strengthen you.

God is love, and all who live in love live in God, and God lives in them.

1 JOHN 4:16 NLT

DAY 11

GENESIS 3:1–10 NLT

The serpent was the shrewdest of all the wild animals the LORD God had made. One day he asked the woman, "Did God really say you must not eat the fruit from any of the trees in the garden?"

"Of course we may eat fruit from the trees in the garden," the woman replied. "It's only the fruit from the tree in the middle of the garden that we are not allowed to eat. God said, 'You must not eat it or even touch it; if you do, you will die.'"

"You won't die!" the serpent replied to the woman. "God knows that your eyes will be opened as soon as you eat it, and you will be like God, knowing both good and evil."

The woman was convinced. She saw that the tree was beautiful and its fruit looked delicious, and she wanted the wisdom it would give her. So she took some of the fruit and ate it. Then she gave some to her husband, who was with her, and he ate it, too. At that moment their eyes were opened, and they suddenly felt shame at their nakedness. So they sewed fig leaves together to cover themselves.

When the cool evening breezes were blowing, the man and his wife heard the LORD God walking about in the garden. So they hid from the LORD God among the trees. Then the LORD God called to the man, "Where are you?"

He replied, "I heard you walking in the garden, so I hid. I was afraid because I was naked."

God's love seeks me out.

EYES TIGHTLY SHUT

He knew he shouldn't have done it. I could clearly see he knew it was wrong: it was written all over his face! As I sat down to discuss his wrongdoing with him, my nephew quickly squeezed his eyes shut. There he sat, thinking with three-year-old logic that if he couldn't see me, then I must not be able to see him. And if he was invisible to me, then he could avoid the conversation (and consequences) he anticipated.

I'm so glad I could see him in that moment. While I couldn't condone his actions, and we needed to talk about it, I really didn't want anything to come between us. I wanted him to look fully into my face and see how much I love him and was eager to forgive him! In that moment, I caught a glimmer of how God might have felt when Adam and Eve broke His trust in the garden of Eden. Realizing their guilt, they tried to hide from God (Genesis 3:10), who could "see" them as plainly as I could see my nephew.

When we realize we've done something wrong, we often want to avoid the consequences. We run from it, conceal it, or close our eyes to the truth. While God will hold us accountable to His righteous standard, He sees us (and seeks us!) because He loves us and offers forgiveness through Jesus Christ.

Kirsten Holmberg

They hid from the Lord God among the trees.

GENESIS 3:8 NLT

Write

Do you ever find yourself running and hiding from God? What distractions or temptations are you drawn to while hiding? How has God gently met you in your place of brokenness?

Connect

What questions would you ask Eve about her experience of Genesis 3?

Is there an area of your life where you may be running and hiding from God right now? Invite Jesus to meet you in that place of brokenness.

DAY 12

JONAH 2:1–9 NLT

Then Jonah prayed to the LORD his God from inside the fish. He said,

"I cried out to the LORD in my great trouble,
and he answered me.
I called to you from the land of the dead,
and LORD, you heard me!
You threw me into the ocean depths,
and I sank down to the heart of the sea.
The mighty waters engulfed me;
I was buried beneath your wild and stormy waves.
Then I said, 'O LORD, you have driven me from your presence.
Yet I will look once more toward your holy Temple.'

"I sank beneath the waves,
and the waters closed over me.
Seaweed wrapped itself around my head.
I sank down to the very roots of the mountains.
I was imprisoned in the earth,
whose gates lock shut forever.
But you, O LORD my God,
snatched me from the jaws of death!
As my life was slipping away,
I remembered the LORD.
And my earnest prayer went out to you
in your holy Temple.
Those who worship false gods
turn their backs on all God's mercies.
But I will offer sacrifices to you with songs of praise,
and I will fulfill all my vows.
For my salvation comes from the LORD alone."

No matter how often I run, God draws me back to Himself.

PURSUED BY LOVE

"I fled Him, down the nights and down the days," opens the famous poem "The Hound of Heaven" by English poet Francis Thompson. Thompson describes Jesus's unceasing pursuit—despite his efforts to hide, or even run away, from God. The poet imagines God speaking to him and saying, "I am He whom thou seekest!"

The pursuing love of God is a central theme of the book of Jonah. The prophet received an assignment to tell the people of Nineveh (notorious enemies of Israel) about their need to turn to God, but instead "Jonah ran away from the Lord" (Jonah 1:3). He secured passage on a ship sailing in the opposite direction of Nineveh, but the vessel was soon overcome by a violent storm. To save the ship's crew, Jonah was thrown overboard before being swallowed by a large fish (1:15–17).

In his own beautiful poem, Jonah recounted that despite his best efforts to run away from God, God pursued him. When Jonah was overcome by his situation and needed to be saved, he cried out to God in prayer and turned toward His love (2:2, 8). God answered and provided rescue not only for Jonah, but for his Assyrian enemies as well (3:10).

As described in both poems, there may be seasons of our lives when we try to run from God. Even then Jesus loves us and is at work guiding us back into restored relationship with Him (1 John 1:9).

Lisa M. Samra

Connect

Take a second look at Jonah's honest prayer. Guided by his prayer, craft your own—openly sharing your challenges, concerns, and unknowns to God and worshiping Him for His merciful grace.

Pray

Where do you feel like you need rescuing right now? Call out to your Savior. He's always willing and available to help.

Write

When, like Jonah, has God lovingly pursued you despite your best efforts to run from Him? What was it like to experience God's relentless love in the face of your brokenness?

For my salvation comes from the LORD alone.

JONAH 2:9 NLT

DAY 13

PROVERBS 27:1–10 NKJV

Do not boast about tomorrow,
For you do not know what a day may bring forth.

Let another man praise you, and not your own mouth;
A stranger, and not your own lips.

A stone is heavy and sand is weighty,
But a fool's wrath is heavier than both of them.

Wrath is cruel and anger a torrent,
But who is able to stand before jealousy?

Open rebuke is better
Than love carefully concealed.

Faithful are the wounds of a friend,
But the kisses of an enemy are deceitful.

A satisfied soul loathes the honeycomb,
But to a hungry soul every bitter thing is sweet.

Like a bird that wanders from its nest
Is a man who wanders from his place.

Ointment and perfume delight the heart,
And the sweetness of a man's friend gives delight by hearty
counsel.

Do not forsake your own friend or your father's friend,
Nor go to your brother's house in the day of your calamity;
Better is a neighbor nearby than a brother far away.

True joy and lasting peace are found in God alone.

WHEN SHARKS WON'T BITE

My children were thrilled, but I felt uneasy. During a vacation, we visited an aquarium where people could pet small sharks kept in a special tank. When I asked the attendant if the creatures ever snapped at fingers, she explained that the sharks had recently been fed and then given extra food. They wouldn't bite because they weren't hungry.

What I learned about shark petting makes sense according to a proverb: "One who is full loathes honey from the comb, but to the hungry even what is bitter tastes sweet" (Proverbs 27:7). Hunger—that sense of inner emptiness—can weaken our discernment as we make decisions. It convinces us that it's okay to settle for anything that fills us up, even if it causes us to take a bite out of someone.

God wants more for us than a life lived at the mercy of our appetites. He wants us to be filled with Christ's love so that everything we do flows from the peace and stability He provides. The constant awareness that we're unconditionally loved gives us confidence. It enables us to be selective as we consider the "sweet" things in life—achievements, possessions, and relationships.

Only a relationship with Jesus gives true satisfaction. May we grasp His incredible love for us so we can be "filled to the measure [with] all the fullness of God" (Ephesians 3:19) for our sake and the sake of others.

Jennifer Benson Schuldt

Write

Can you remember a time when you felt empty or dry? What was that experience like, and what would you like Jesus to know about it?

A satisfied soul loathes the honeycomb, but to a hungry soul every bitter thing is sweet.

PROVERBS 27:7 NKJV

Connect

What new, fresh ways in this season do you want to connect with God and to serve others?

Pray

Invite Jesus to meet you wherever you are today—whether full of joy or weary—to reassure you of just how much He cares for you.

DAY 14

JOEL 2:18–27

Then the LORD was jealous for his
land
and took pity on his people.

The LORD replied to them:

"I am sending you grain, new wine
and olive oil,
enough to satisfy you fully;
never again will I make you
an object of scorn to the nations.

"I will drive the northern horde far
from you,
pushing it into a parched and
barren land;
its eastern ranks will drown in the
Dead Sea
and its western ranks in the
Mediterranean Sea.
And its stench will go up;
its smell will rise."

Surely he has done great things!
Do not be afraid, land of Judah;
be glad and rejoice.
Surely the LORD has done great
things!
Do not be afraid, you wild
animals,
for the pastures in the wilderness
are becoming green.
The trees are bearing their fruit;
the fig tree and the vine yield
their riches.

Be glad, people of Zion,
rejoice in the LORD your God,
for he has given you the autumn
rains
because he is faithful.
He sends you abundant showers,
both autumn and spring rains, as
before.
The threshing floors will be filled
with grain;
the vats will overflow with new
wine and oil.

"I will repay you for the years the
locusts have eaten—
the great locust and the young
locust,
the other locusts and the locust
swarm—
my great army that I sent among
you.
You will have plenty to eat, until
you are full,
and you will praise the name of
the LORD your God,
who has worked wonders for
you;
never again will my people be
shamed.
Then you will know that I am in
Israel,
that I am the LORD your God,
and that there is no other;
never again will my people be
shamed."

God's love restores.

RESTORED

A 2003 infestation of Mormon crickets caused more than twenty-five million dollars in lost crops. The crickets came in such numbers that people couldn't so much as take a step without finding one underfoot. The grasshopper-like insect, named for attacking the crops of the Utah pioneers in 1848, can eat an astounding thirty-eight pounds of plant material in their lifetimes, despite being merely two to three inches long. The impact of infestations on farmers' livelihoods—and the overall economy of a state or country—can be devastating.

The Old Testament prophet Joel described a horde of similar insects ravaging the entire nation of Judah as a consequence for their collective disobedience. He foretold an invasion of locusts (a metaphor for a foreign army, in the minds of some Bible scholars) like nothing previous generations had seen (Joel 1:2). The locusts would lay waste to everything in their path, driving the people into famine and poverty. If, however, the people would turn from their sinful ways and ask God for forgiveness, Joel says the Lord would "repay [them] for the years the locusts have eaten" (2:25).

We too can learn from Judah's lesson: like insects, our wrongdoings eat away at the fruitful, fragrant life God intended for us. When we turn toward Him, and away from our past choices, He promises to remove our shame and restore us to an abundant life in Him.

Kirsten Holmberg

Where in your life do you sense it might be wise to change direction? Invite Jesus into the conversation.

Connect

Write down a word or phrase from Joel 2:18–27, today's Bible passage, that grabs your attention. Why does it stand out to you?

In what ways have you received a second chance? Let yourself feel gratitude to God for them.

I will repay you for the years the locusts have eaten.

JOEL 2:25

DAY 15

PROVERBS 17:19–22 ESV

Whoever loves transgression loves strife;
he who makes his door high seeks destruction.
A man of crooked heart does not discover good,
and one with a dishonest tongue falls into calamity.
He who sires a fool gets himself sorrow,
and the father of a fool has no joy.
A joyful heart is good medicine,
but a crushed spirit dries up the bones.

Laughter is "good medicine" for your spirit.

GOOD MEDICINE

Greg and Elizabeth have a regular "Joke Night" with their four school-age children. Each child brings several jokes they've read or heard (or made up themselves!) during the week to tell at the dinner table. This tradition has created joyful memories of fun shared around the table. Greg and Elizabeth even noticed the laughter was healthy for their children, lifting their spirits on difficult days.

The benefit of joyful conversation around the dinner table was observed by C. S. Lewis, who wrote, "The sun looks down on nothing half so good as a household laughing together over a meal."

The wisdom of fostering a joyful heart is found in Proverbs 17:22 (ESV), where we read, "A joyful heart is good medicine, but a crushed spirit dries up the bones." The proverb offers a "prescription" to stimulate health and healing—allowing joy to fill our hearts, a medicine that costs little and yields great results.

We all need this biblical prescription. When we bring joy into our conversations, it can put a disagreement into perspective. It can help us to experience peace, even after a stressful test at school or a difficult day at work. Laughter among family and friends can create a safe place where we both know and feel that we're loved.

Do you need to incorporate more laughter into your life as "good medicine" for your spirit? Remember, you have encouragement from Scripture to cultivate a cheerful heart.

Lisa M. Samra

A joyful heart is good medicine, but a crushed spirit dries up the bones.

PROVERBS 17:22 ESV

Write

Where in your life do you need to let loose and laugh more?

Connect

Take a few moments to let go and just relax and be playful—even silly—in God's presence. What's this like for you? Does anything surprise you?

Pray

Imagine looking at Jesus's face and He is smiling with love at you! How does it feel knowing your Savior delights, and finds joy, in you?

GENESIS 1:26–31 NLT

Then God said, "Let us make human beings in our image, to be like us. They will reign over the fish in the sea, the birds in the sky, the livestock, all the wild animals on the earth, and the small animals that scurry along the ground."

> So God created human beings in his own image.
> In the image of God he created them;
> male and female he created them.

Then God blessed them and said, "Be fruitful and multiply. Fill the earth and govern it. Reign over the fish in the sea, the birds in the sky, and all the animals that scurry along the ground."

Then God said, "Look! I have given you every seed-bearing plant throughout the earth and all the fruit trees for your food. And I have given every green plant as food for all the wild animals, the birds in the sky, and the small animals that scurry along the ground—everything that has life." And that is what happened.

Then God looked over all he had made, and he saw that it was very good!

And evening passed and morning came, marking the sixth day.

I am an image-bearer of God.

IN GOD'S IMAGE

When her beautiful brown skin started losing its color, a young woman felt frightened, as if she were disappearing or losing her "self." With heavy makeup, she covered up "my spots," as she called them—patches of lighter skin caused by a condition called vitiligo. It's a loss of skin pigment, melanin, which gives skin its tone.

Then one day, she asked herself: Why hide? Relying on God's strength to accept herself, she stopped wearing heavy makeup. Soon she began gaining attention for her self-confidence. Eventually she became the first spokesmodel with vitiligo for a global cosmetics brand.

"It's such a blessing," she told a TV news host, adding that her faith, family, and friends are the ways she finds encouragement.

This woman's story invites us to remember that we each are created in God's image. "God created mankind in his own image, in the image of God he created them; male and female he created them" (Genesis 1:27). No matter what we look like on the outside, all of us are image-bearers of God. As His created persons, we reflect His glory; and as believers in Jesus, we are being transformed to represent Him in the world.

Do you struggle to love the skin you're in? Today, look in the mirror and smile for God. He created you in His image.

Patricia Raybon

Connect

Create a list of things about yourself that you like or don't like and invite God's fresh perspective about each one.

Pray

Bring to God an area of your life where you struggle to feel confident or worthy.

Write

Let the beautiful truth that you're made in God's image sink in and draw you into a conversation with your loving Creator.

God created human beings in his own image. In the image of God he created them; male and female he created them.

GENESIS 1:27 NLT

JUDGES 6:1, 11–16

The Israelites did evil in the eyes of the Lord, and for seven years he gave them into the hands of the Midianites. . . .

The angel of the Lord came and sat down under the oak in Ophrah that belonged to Joash the Abiezrite, where his son Gideon was threshing wheat in a winepress to keep it from the Midianites. When the angel of the Lord appeared to Gideon, he said, "The Lord is with you, mighty warrior."

"Pardon me, my lord," Gideon replied, "but if the Lord is with us, why has all this happened to us? Where are all his wonders that our ancestors told us about when they said, 'Did not the Lord bring us up out of Egypt?' But now the Lord has abandoned us and given us into the hand of Midian."

The Lord turned to him and said, "Go in the strength you have and save Israel out of Midian's hand. Am I not sending you?"

"Pardon me, my lord," Gideon replied, "but how can I save Israel? My clan is the weakest in Manasseh, and I am the least in my family."

The Lord answered, "I will be with you, and you will strike down all the Midianites, leaving none alive."

My self-worth and identity come from being a child of God.

WALK LIKE A WARRIOR

Eighteen-year-old Emma faithfully talks about Jesus on social media, even though bullies have criticized her joy and enthusiastic love for Christ. Some have attacked her with remarks about her physical appearance. Others have suggested a lack of intelligence because of her devotion to God. Though the unkind words cut deep into Emma's heart, she continues to spread the gospel with bold faith and love for Jesus and others. Sometimes, though, she's tempted to believe her identity and worth are determined by the criticism of others. When that happens, she asks God for help, prays for her persecutors, meditates on the words of Scripture, and perseveres with Spirit-empowered courage and confidence.

Gideon faced fierce tormentors—the Midianites (Judges 6:1–10). Though God called him a "mighty warrior," Gideon struggled to let go of his doubt, self-imposed limitations, and insecurities (vv. 11–15). On more than one occasion, he questioned the Lord's presence and his own qualifications, but eventually surrendered in faith.

When we trust God, we can live like we believe what He says about us is true. Even when persecution tempts us to doubt our identity, our loving Father confirms His presence and fights on our behalf. He affirms we can walk like mighty warriors armed with His absolute love, guarded by His endless grace, and secured in His reliable truth.

Xochitl Dixon

When the angel of the LORD appeared to Gideon, he said, "The LORD is with you, mighty warrior."

JUDGES 6:12

Write

What's one lie you're tempted to believe today, and one truth you need to cling to?

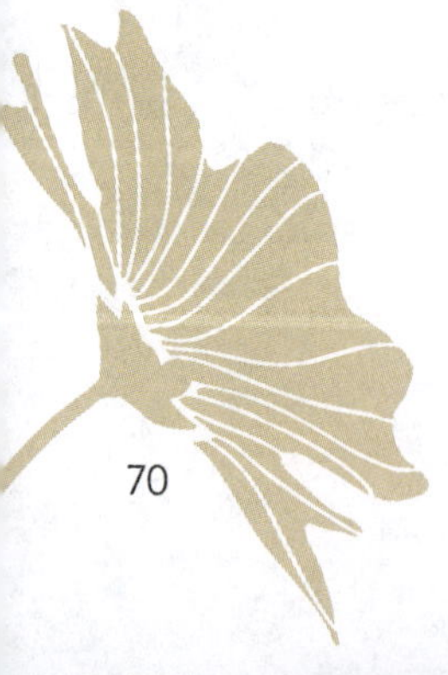

Connect

If God were to say to you, as He did to Gideon, "The Lord is with you, mighty warrior" (Judges 6:12), what emotions and thoughts would come up? How would you respond to His words?

Invite Jesus to speak life and truth over a lie that is dragging you down.

DAY 18

1 SAMUEL 18:1–4; 19:1–6 ESV

As soon as he had finished speaking to Saul, the soul of Jonathan was knit to the soul of David, and Jonathan loved him as his own soul. And Saul took him that day and would not let him return to his father's house. Then Jonathan made a covenant with David, because he loved him as his own soul. And Jonathan stripped himself of the robe that was on him and gave it to David, and his armor, and even his sword and his bow and his belt. . . .

And Saul spoke to Jonathan his son and to all his servants, that they should kill David. But Jonathan, Saul's son, delighted much in David. And Jonathan told David, "Saul my father seeks to kill you. Therefore be on your guard in the morning. Stay in a secret place and hide yourself. And I will go out and stand beside my father in the field where you are, and I will speak to my father about you. And if I learn anything I will tell you." And Jonathan spoke well of David to Saul his father and said to him, "Let not the king sin against his servant David, because he has not sinned against you, and because his deeds have brought good to you. For he took his life in his hand and he struck down the Philistine, and the Lord worked a great salvation for all Israel. You saw it, and rejoiced. Why then will you sin against innocent blood by killing David without cause?" And Saul listened to the voice of Jonathan. Saul swore, "As the Lord lives, he shall not be put to death."

My friendship with God provides me indescribable freedom and complete safety.

TRUE FRIENDS

In middle school, I had a "sometimes friend." We were "buddies" at our small church (where I was nearly the only girl her age), and we occasionally hung out together outside of school. But at school, it was a different story. If she met me by herself, she might say hello, but only if no one else was around. Realizing this, I rarely tried to gain her attention within school walls. I knew the limits of our friendship.

We've probably all experienced the pain of disappointingly one-sided or narrow friendships. But there's another kind of friendship, one that extends beyond all boundaries. It's the kind of friendship we have with kindred spirits who are committed to sharing life's journey with us.

David and Jonathan were such friends. Jonathan was "one in spirit" with David and loved him "as himself" (1 Samuel 18:1–3). Although Jonathan would have been next in line to rule after his father Saul's death, he was loyal to David, God's chosen replacement. Jonathan even helped David to evade two of Saul's plots to kill him (19:1–6; 20:1–42).

Despite all odds, Jonathan and David remained friends, pointing to the truth of Proverbs 17:17: "A friend loves at all times." Their faithful friendship also gives us a glimpse of the loving relationship God has with us (John 3:16; 15:15). Through friendships like theirs, our understanding of God's love is deepened.

Alyson Kieda

Reflect on a quality you genuinely need in a friend in this season and talk with Jesus about your deep need.

Connect

What are your hopes and desires for your friendship with God right now? What might you like to say to God about those longings?

What do you admire about Jonathan and David's friendship? How might you emulate their loyalty, support, and care for each other in your own relationships?

A friend loves at all times.

PROVERBS 17:17

DAY 19

LUKE 8:40–48

Now when Jesus returned, a crowd welcomed him, for they were all expecting him. Then a man named Jairus, a synagogue leader, came and fell at Jesus' feet, pleading with him to come to his house because his only daughter, a girl of about twelve, was dying.

As Jesus was on his way, the crowds almost crushed him. And a woman was there who had been subject to bleeding for twelve years, but no one could heal her. She came up behind him and touched the edge of his cloak, and immediately her bleeding stopped.

"Who touched me?" Jesus asked.

When they all denied it, Peter said, "Master, the people are crowding and pressing against you."

But Jesus said, "Someone touched me; I know that power has gone out from me."

Then the woman, seeing that she could not go unnoticed, came trembling and fell at his feet. In the presence of all the people, she told why she had touched him and how she had been instantly healed. Then he said to her, "Daughter, your faith has healed you. Go in peace."

Jesus asks me to trust Him and to never give up hope.

NEVER GIVE UP HOPE

When my friend received a diagnosis of cancer, the doctor advised her to get her affairs in order. She called me, sobbing, worried about her husband and young children. I shared her urgent prayer request with our mutual friends. We rejoiced when a second doctor encouraged her to never give up hope and confirmed his team would do all they could to help. Though some days were harder than others, she focused on God instead of the odds stacked against her. She never gave up.

My friend's persevering faith reminds me of the desperate woman in Luke 8. Weary from twelve years of ongoing suffering, disappointment, and isolation, she approached Jesus from behind and stretched her hand toward the hem of His robe. Her immediate healing followed her act of faith: persistently hoping—believing Jesus was able to do what others couldn't—no matter how impossible her situation seemed (vv. 43–44).

We may experience pain that feels endless, situations that appear hopeless, or waiting that seems unbearable. We may endure moments when the odds against us are stacked high and wide. We may not experience the healing we long for as we continue trusting Christ. But even then, Jesus invites us to keep reaching for Him, to trust Him and never give up hope, and to believe He is always able, always trustworthy, and always within reach.

Xochitl Dixon

[Jesus] said to her, "Daughter, your faith has healed you. Go in peace."

LUKE 8:48

Write

What part of the story from Luke 8:40–48, today's Bible passage, jumps out at you? Why?

Connect

Imagine hearing Jesus say to you: "Daughter, your faith has healed you. Go in peace." What feelings rise up in you? Is there anything you'd like Jesus to know?

Pray

Let Jesus speak into a struggle you've been carrying for a long time.

DAY 20

JOHN 14:15–21 ESV

If you love me, you will keep my commandments. And I will ask the Father, and he will give you another Helper, to be with you forever, even the Spirit of truth, whom the world cannot receive, because it neither sees him nor knows him. You know him, for he dwells with you and will be in you.

I will not leave you as orphans; I will come to you. Yet a little while and the world will see me no more, but you will see me. Because I live, you also will live. In that day you will know that I am in my Father, and you in me, and I in you. Whoever has my commandments and keeps them, he it is who loves me. And he who loves me will be loved by my Father, and I will love him and manifest myself to him.

The Holy Spirit within me empowers me to stay in step with God's purposes.

DO THE NEXT THING

When was the last time you felt compelled to help someone, only to let the moment pass without a response? In *The 10-Second Rule*, Clare De Graaf suggests that daily impressions can be one of the ways God calls us to a deeper spiritual walk, a life of obedience prompted by love for Him. *The 10-Second Rule* encourages you to simply "do the next thing you're reasonably certain Jesus wants you to do," and to do it right away "before you change your mind."

Jesus says, "If you love me, you will keep my commandments" (John 14:15 ESV). We might think, I do love Him, but how can I be certain of His will and follow it? In His wisdom, Jesus has provided what we need to better understand and follow the wisdom found in the Bible. He once said, "I will ask the Father, and he will give you another Helper, to be with you forever, even the Spirit of truth" (vv. 16–17 ESV). It's by the work of the Spirit, who is with us and in us, that we can learn to obey Jesus and "keep [His] commandments" (v. 15 ESV)—responding to the promptings experienced throughout our day (v. 17).

In the big and little things, the Spirit motivates us to confidently do by faith what will honor God and reveal our love for Him and others (v. 21).

Ruth O'Reilly-Smith

Connect

What are your questions about the Holy Spirit?

Pray

Where are you feeling called to serve, give, or take action today? Invite the Holy Spirit into the conversation.

Write

Journal about a time you felt prompted to take action. What was that like for you? If you were motivated to act, was it exhilarating, freeing, scary, or ______________________________ [fill in the blank] to respond?

If you love me, you will keep my commandments.

JOHN 14:15 ESV

DAY 21

JEREMIAH 15:15–21

Lord, you understand;
remember me and care for me.
Avenge me on my persecutors.
You are long-suffering—do not take
me away;
think of how I suffer reproach
for your sake.
When your words came, I ate them;
they were my joy and my heart's
delight,
for I bear your name,
Lord God Almighty.
I never sat in the company of
revelers,
never made merry with them;
I sat alone because your hand was
on me
and you had filled me with
indignation.
Why is my pain unending
and my wound grievous and
incurable?
You are to me like a deceptive
brook,
like a spring that fails.

Therefore this is what the Lord says:

"If you repent, I will restore you
that you may serve me;
if you utter worthy, not worthless,
words,
you will be my spokesman.
Let this people turn to you,
but you must not turn to them.
I will make you a wall to this
people,
a fortified wall of bronze;
they will fight against you
but will not overcome you,
for I am with you
to rescue and save you,"
declares the Lord.
"I will save you from the hands
of the wicked
and deliver you from the grasp of
the cruel."

When I call out to God, He listens and hears my cry.

HUNGRY FOR GOD

A new believer in Jesus was desperate to read the Bible. However, he'd lost his eyesight and both hands in an explosion. When he heard about a woman who read Braille with her lips, he tried to do the same—only to discover that the nerve endings of his lips had also been destroyed. Later, he was filled with joy when he discovered that he could feel the Braille characters with his tongue! He had found a way to read and enjoy the Scriptures.

Joy and delight were the emotions the prophet Jeremiah experienced when he received God's words. "When your words came, I ate them," he said; "they were my joy and my heart's delight" (Jeremiah 15:16). Unlike the people of Judah who despised His words (8:9), Jeremiah had been obedient and rejoiced in them. His obedience, however, also led to the prophet being rejected by his own people and persecuted unfairly (v. 17).

Some of us may have experienced something similar. We once read the Bible with joy, but obedience to God led to suffering and rejection from others. Like Jeremiah, we can bring our confusion to God. He answered Jeremiah by repeating the promise He gave him when He first called him to be a prophet (vv. 19–21; see 1:18–19). God reminded him that He never lets His people down. We can have this same confidence too. He's faithful and will never abandon us.

Poh Fang Chia

Write

When have you experienced encouragement and refreshment in God's Word? What was that like for you, and how did it draw you close to God?

When your words came, I ate them; they were my joy and my heart's delight.

JEREMIAH 15:16

Connect

How do you feel invited to wholly surrender and live freely for Christ in this season? Let Jesus speak into your sense of calling.

Pray

Bring to mind—and meditate on—a favorite Scripture passage. Invite Jesus to open your heart and mind to receive from it fresh insights and encouragement.

DAY 22

ECCLESIASTES 1:3–11 NKJV

What profit has a man from all his labor
In which he toils under the sun?
One generation passes away, and another generation comes;
But the earth abides forever.
The sun also rises, and the sun goes down,
And hastens to the place where it arose.
The wind goes toward the south,
And turns around to the north;
The wind whirls about continually,
And comes again on its circuit.
All the rivers run into the sea,
Yet the sea is not full;
To the place from which the rivers come,
There they return again.
All things are full of labor;
Man cannot express it.
The eye is not satisfied with seeing,
Nor the ear filled with hearing.

That which has been is what will be,
That which is done is what will be done,
And there is nothing new under the sun.
Is there anything of which it may be said,
"See, this is new"?
It has already been in ancient times before us.
There is no remembrance of former things,
Nor will there be any remembrance of things that are to come
By those who will come after.

God sees and values the ordinary, seemingly mundane parts of my life.

KNOCKING DOWN PINS

I was intrigued when I noticed a tattoo of a bowling ball knocking down pins on my friend Erin's ankle. Erin was inspired to get this unique tattoo after listening to Sara Groves's song, "Setting Up the Pins." The clever lyrics encourage listeners to find joy in the repetitive, routine tasks that sometimes feel as pointless as manually setting up bowling pins over and over again, only to have someone knock them down.

Laundry. Cooking. Mowing the lawn. Life seems full of tasks that, once completed, have to be done again—and again. This isn't a new struggle. The ancient book of Ecclesiastes opens with the author complaining about the endless cycles of daily human life as futile (1:2–3), even meaningless. He says, "What has been will be again, what has been done will be done again" (v. 9).

Yet, like my friend, the writer was able to regain a sense of joy and meaning by remembering that our ultimate fulfillment comes as we "fear [reverence] God and keep his commandments" (12:13 NKJV). There's comfort in knowing that God values even the ordinary, seemingly mundane aspects of life and will reward our faithfulness (v. 14).

What are the "pins" you're continually setting up? In those times when repetitive tasks begin to feel tiring, may we take a moment to offer each task to God as an offering of love. *Lisa M. Samra*

Pray

Think about a mundane or overwhelming task
and ask to see it from God's perspective.

Connect

Your work is worship. Visualize giving each of your tasks and responsibilities to God. As you do so, what emotions and thoughts come up? How does the exercise reveal God's loving care?

What tasks energize and fill you up—and which drain and exhaust you? Invite Jesus into a conversation about your health and wholeness because Christ cares deeply about your well-being.

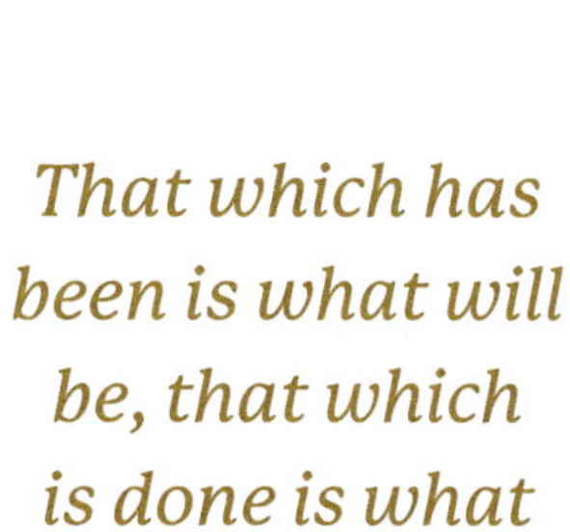

That which has been is what will be, that which is done is what will be done.

ECCLESIASTES 1:9 NKJV

DAY 23

1 SAMUEL 30:1–6, 18–19

David and his men reached Ziklag on the third day. Now the Amalekites had raided the Negev and Ziklag. They had attacked Ziklag and burned it, and had taken captive the women and everyone else in it, both young and old. They killed none of them, but carried them off as they went on their way.

When David and his men reached Ziklag, they found it destroyed by fire and their wives and sons and daughters taken captive. So David and his men wept aloud until they had no strength left to weep. David's two wives had been captured—Ahinoam of Jezreel and Abigail, the widow of Nabal of Carmel. David was greatly distressed because the men were talking of stoning him; each one was bitter in spirit because of his sons and daughters. But David found strength in the Lord his God. . . .

David recovered everything the Amalekites had taken, including his two wives. Nothing was missing: young or old, boy or girl, plunder or anything else they had taken. David brought everything back.

God is my strength and defender.

RECOVERING WHAT'S LOST

At the phone store, the young pastor steeled himself for bad news. His smart phone, accidentally dropped during our Bible class, was a total loss, right? Actually, no. The store clerk recovered all of the pastor's data, including his Bible videos and photos. She also recovered "every photo I'd ever deleted," he said. The store also "replaced my broken phone with a brand-new phone." As he said, "I recovered all I had lost and more."

David once led his own recovery mission after an attack by the vicious Amalekites. Spurned by Philistine rulers, David and his army discovered the Amalekites had raided and burned down their town of Ziklag, taking captive "the women and everyone else in it," including all their wives and children (1 Samuel 30:2–3). "So David and his men wept aloud until they had no strength left to weep" (v. 4). The soldiers were so bitter with their leader David that they talked of "stoning him" (v. 6).

"But David found strength in the Lord his God" (v. 6). As God promised, David pursued the Amalekites and "recovered everything the Amalekites had taken. . . . Nothing was missing: young or old, boy or girl, plunder or anything else they had taken. David brought everything back" (vv. 18–19). As we face spiritual attacks that rob us even of hope, may we find renewed strength in God. He will be with us in every challenge of life.

Patricia Raybon

But David found strength in the Lord his God.

1 SAMUEL 30:6

Write

Is there someone in your life like David, who finds courage and strength in God amid their challenges? Consider reaching out to them to encourage them.

Connect

If you could interview someone from today's Bible story, 1 Samuel 30, who would it be? What questions would you ask? Journal about what comes to mind from this "conversation."

Pray

In what circumstance do you feel alone and struggle to know what to do next? Cry out to Jesus with the assurance that He cares for you.

DAY 24

1 THESSALONIANS 5:11–18 NKJV

Therefore comfort each other and edify one another, just as you also are doing.

And we urge you, brethren, to recognize those who labor among you, and are over you in the Lord and admonish you, and to esteem them very highly in love for their work's sake. Be at peace among yourselves.

Now we exhort you, brethren, warn those who are unruly, comfort the fainthearted, uphold the weak, be patient with all. See that no one renders evil for evil to anyone, but always pursue what is good both for yourselves and for all.

Rejoice always, pray without ceasing, in everything give thanks; for this is the will of God in Christ Jesus for you.

The church family is called to lift one another up, not tear each other down.

PLIGHT OF THE CRAWDADS

When my cousin invited me to join him to fish for crawdads (crayfish), I couldn't help but be excited. I grinned when he handed me a plastic pail. "No lid?"

"You won't need one," he said, picking up the fishing rods and the small bag of chicken chunks we'd use for bait.

Later, as I watched the small crustaceans climbing over one another in a futile attempt to escape the almost-full bucket, I realized why we wouldn't need a lid. Whenever one crawdad reached the rim, the others would pull it back down.

The plight of the crawdads reminds me how destructive it is to be selfishly concerned about our own gain instead of the benefit of a whole community. Paul understood the need for uplifting, interdependent relationships when he wrote to the believers in Thessalonica.

Commending their caring community (v. 11), Paul spurred them toward even more loving and peaceful relationships (vv. 13–15). By striving to create a culture of forgiveness, kindness, and compassion, their relationships with God and others would be strengthened (vv. 15, 23).

The church can grow and witness for Christ through this kind of loving unity. When believers honor God, committing to lift others up instead of pulling them down, we and our communities thrive.

Xochitl Dixon

Connect

Look at just a few ways the church is called to gently uplift and support one another. What encouragement about community life in the passage below especially speaks to you in this season? Why?

> Get along among yourselves, each of you doing your part. Our counsel is that you warn the freeloaders to get a move on. Gently encourage the stragglers, and reach out for the exhausted, pulling them to their feet. Be patient with each person, attentive to individual needs. And be careful that when you get on each other's nerves you don't snap at each other. Look for the best in each other, and always do your best to bring it out. (1 Thessalonians 5:13–15 MSG)

Pray

Is there someone frequently on your mind and heart? Let Jesus speak life and encouragement over that relationship.

Write

Can you remember a time when you felt a powerful sense of belonging? What about that experience deeply resonates with you today?

Always pursue what is good both for yourselves and for all.

1 THESSALONIANS 5:15 NKJV

DAY 25

1 KINGS 17:2–6

Then the word of the LORD came to Elijah: "Leave here, turn eastward and hide in the Kerith Ravine, east of the Jordan. You will drink from the brook, and I have directed the ravens to supply you with food there."

So he did what the LORD had told him. He went to the Kerith Ravine, east of the Jordan, and stayed there. The ravens brought him bread and meat in the morning and bread and meat in the evening, and he drank from the brook.

Out of His abundant provision,
God will meet my every need.

CHIRPY

For twelve years, Chirpy, a seagull, has made daily visits to a man who'd helped him heal from a broken leg. John wooed Chirpy to himself with dog biscuits and was then able to nurse him back to health. Though Chirpy only resides in Instow Beach in Devon, England, between September and March, he and John Sumner find each other easily—Chirpy flies straight to him when he arrives at the beach each day, though he doesn't approach any other human. It's an uncommon relationship, to be sure.

John and Chirpy's bond reminds me of another uncommon relationship between man and bird. When Elijah, one of God's prophets, was sent into the wilderness to "hide in the Kerith Ravine" during a time of drought, God said he was to drink from the brook, and He'd send ravens to supply him with food (1 Kings 17:3–4). Despite the difficult circumstances and surroundings, Elijah would have his needs for food and water met. Ravens were unlikely caterers—naturally feeding on unseemly meals themselves—yet they brought Elijah wholesome food.

It may not surprise us that a man would help a bird, but when birds provide for a man with "bread and meat in the morning and bread and meat in the evening," it can only be explained by God's power and care (v. 6). Like Elijah, we too can trust in His provision for us.

Kirsten Holmberg

The ravens brought him bread and meat in the morning and bread and meat in the evening, and he drank from the brook.

1 KINGS 17:6

Write

Can you remember a time when your deep needs were met in unexpected or even miraculous ways? What was that experience like, and how did you sense God's loving care?

Connect

What part of today's story from 1 Kings 17:2–6 captures your attention? Why?

Pray

Invite Jesus to meet a present need, trusting that He is willing, able, and ready to provide.

DAY 26

HEBREWS 1:8–12

But about the Son he says,

> "Your throne, O God, will last for ever and ever;
> a scepter of justice will be the scepter of your kingdom.
> You have loved righteousness and hated wickedness;
> therefore God, your God, has set you above your companions
> by anointing you with the oil of joy."

He also says,

> "In the beginning, Lord, you laid the foundations of the earth,
> and the heavens are the work of your hands.
> They will perish, but you remain;
> they will all wear out like a garment.
> You will roll them up like a robe;
> like a garment they will be changed.
> But you remain the same,
> and your years will never end."

Joy was at the heart of
Jesus's mission.

THE SMILING JESUS

If you were to play the part of Jesus in a movie, how would you approach the role? That was the challenge faced by Bruce Marchiano, who played Jesus in *The Visual Bible: Matthew*. Knowing that millions of viewers would draw conclusions about Jesus based on his work, the weight of getting Christ "right" felt overwhelming. He fell to his knees in prayer and begged Jesus for—well, for Jesus.

Bruce gained insight from the first chapter of Hebrews, where the writer tells us how God the Father set the Son apart by anointing Him "with the oil of joy" (1:9). This kind of joy is one of celebration—a gladness of connection to the Father expressed wholeheartedly. Such joy ruled in Jesus's heart throughout His life. As Hebrews 12:2 describes it, "For the joy set before him he endured the cross, scorning its shame, and sat down at the right hand of the throne of God."

Taking his cue from this scriptural expression, Bruce offered a uniquely joy-filled portrayal of his Savior. As a result, he became known as "the smiling Jesus." We too can dare to fall to our knees and "beg Jesus for Jesus." May He so fill us with His character that people around us see the expression of His love in us.

Elisa Morgan

Imagine Jesus smiling at you. What's it like to receive God's attention and care?

Connect

Jesus felt deeply, expressing the full range of human emotion. Which example of Jesus's emotional life especially connects with you today?

Joy: Jesus wants His deep joy to overflow in us: "I have told you this so that my joy may be in you and that your joy may be complete" (John 15:11).

Grief: The night of His arrest, Jesus said to His disciples: "My soul is overwhelmed with sorrow to the point of death. Stay here and keep watch with me" (Matthew 26:38).

Anger: At the temple, Jesus drove out vendors because He was enraged that in this space dedicated to worship, people idolized money: "Get these out of here!" Jesus said. "Stop turning my Father's house into a market!" (John 2:16).

Compassion: Jesus saw a widow mourning the loss of her only son, and "his heart went out to her" and He said, "Don't cry" (Luke 7:13). Moved by compassion, Jesus brought her son back to life.

Amazement: Jesus was "amazed" (Matthew 8:10) by the faith of a Roman centurion, who trusted Jesus to heal his servant from afar.

Write

When picturing Jesus, what emotion do you associate with Him? Why?

God . . . has set you above your companions by anointing you with the oil of joy.

HEBREWS 1:9

DAY 27

1 JOHN 3:16–18 NLT

We know what real love is because Jesus gave up his life for us. So we also ought to give up our lives for our brothers and sisters. If someone has enough money to live well and sees a brother or sister in need but shows no compassion—how can God's love be in that person?

Dear children, let's not merely say that we love each other; let us show the truth by our actions.

Serving others can help me understand God's heart.

RELENTLESS LOVE

Heidi and Jeff came home from an overseas work assignment in a hot climate and settled for several months near family in the state of Michigan—just in time for winter. This would be the first time many of their ten children had seen the natural beauty of snow.

But winter weather in Michigan requires a lot of warm outerwear, including coats, mittens, and boots. For a large family, it would be quite an expensive undertaking just to outfit them for the bitterly cold months ahead. But God provided. First, a neighbor brought over footwear, then snow pants, then hats and gloves. Then, a friend urged others at her church to collect a variety of warm clothes in all twelve sizes for each member of the family. By the time the snow arrived, the family had exactly what they needed.

One of the ways we serve God is by serving those in need. First John 3:16–18 encourages us to help others from the abundance of our own possessions. Serving helps us to be more like Jesus as we begin to love and see people as He does.

God often uses His children to fulfill needs and to answer prayers. And as we serve others, our own hearts are encouraged as we encourage those we serve. As a result, our own faith will grow as God equips us for service in new ways (v. 18).

Cindy Hess Kasper

Dear children, let's not merely say that we love each other; let us show the truth by our actions.

1 JOHN 3:18 NLT

Write

When have you felt God's care through someone else? How did that experience draw you closer to God?

Connect

Brainstorm local, national, and international opportunities to serve, give, and love others. Invite the Holy Spirit to highlight one option to pursue or learn more about.

Who has lifted you up, encouraged you, and walked with you in a hard season? Offer up a prayer of thanks for them.

DAY 28

PHILIPPIANS 4:10–20

I rejoiced greatly in the Lord that at last you renewed your concern for me. Indeed, you were concerned, but you had no opportunity to show it. I am not saying this because I am in need, for I have learned to be content whatever the circumstances. I know what it is to be in need, and I know what it is to have plenty. I have learned the secret of being content in any and every situation, whether well fed or hungry, whether living in plenty or in want. I can do all this through him who gives me strength.

Yet it was good of you to share in my troubles. Moreover, as you Philippians know, in the early days of your acquaintance with the gospel, when I set out from Macedonia, not one church shared with me in the matter of giving and receiving, except you only; for even when I was in Thessalonica, you sent me aid more than once when I was in need. Not that I desire your gifts; what I desire is that more be credited to your account. I have received full payment and have more than enough. I am amply supplied, now that I have received from Epaphroditus the gifts you sent. They are a fragrant offering, an acceptable sacrifice, pleasing to God. And my God will meet all your needs according to the riches of his glory in Christ Jesus.

To our God and Father be glory for ever and ever. Amen.

Lasting contentment is found in trusting God to meet my every need.

WHACK-A-MOLE

You might know what it's like. The bills keep arriving after a medical procedure—from the anesthesiologist, the surgeon, the lab, the facility. Jason experienced this after an emergency surgery. He complained, "We owe thousands of dollars after insurance. If only we can get these bills paid, then life will be good and I'll be content! I feel like I'm playing the arcade game Whack-a-Mole"—where plastic moles pop up from their holes, and the player hits them wildly with a mallet.

Life comes at us like that at times. The apostle Paul certainly could relate. He said, "I know what it is to be in need," yet he'd "learned the secret of being content in any and every situation" (Philippians 4:12). His secret? "I can do all this through him who gives me strength" (v. 13). When I was going through a particularly discontented time, I read this on a greeting card: "If it isn't here, where is it?" That was a powerful reminder that if I'm not content here and now, what makes me think I'd be content if only I were in another situation?

How do we learn to rest in Jesus? Maybe it's a matter of focus. Of enjoying and being thankful for the good. Of learning more about a faithful Father. Of growing in trust and patience. Of recognizing that life is about God and not me. Of asking Him to teach me contentment in Him.

Anne Cetas

Connect

Circle or underline a word or phrase from Philippians 4:10–20, today's Bible reading, that stirs your heart and mind. Why does it resonate with you?

Pray

The secret to contentment is this: "I can do all this through him who gives me strength" (Philippians 4:13). Where do you feel incomplete today? Let Jesus freely offer His strength to meet you right there.

The apostle Paul said, "Godliness with contentment is great gain" (1 Timothy 6:6). What strikes you about this refreshing truth?

Godliness with contentment is great gain.

1 TIMOTHY 6:6

JOHN 15:1–11 NKJV

I am the true vine, and My Father is the vinedresser. Every branch in Me that does not bear fruit He takes away; and every branch that bears fruit He prunes, that it may bear more fruit. You are already clean because of the word which I have spoken to you. Abide in Me, and I in you. As the branch cannot bear fruit of itself, unless it abides in the vine, neither can you, unless you abide in Me.

I am the vine, you are the branches. He who abides in Me, and I in him, bears much fruit; for without Me you can do nothing. If anyone does not abide in Me, he is cast out as a branch and is withered; and they gather them and throw them into the fire, and they are burned. If you abide in Me, and My words abide in you, you will ask what you desire, and it shall be done for you. By this My Father is glorified, that you bear much fruit; so you will be My disciples.

As the Father loved Me, I also have loved you; abide in My love. If you keep My commandments, you will abide in My love, just as I have kept My Father's commandments and abide in His love.

These things I have spoken to you, that My joy may remain in you, and that your joy may be full.

True significance comes from relying on God's strength, not my own.

A DIVINE DUET

At a children's music recital, I watched a teacher and student seat themselves in front of a piano. Before their duet began, the teacher leaned over and whispered some last-minute instructions. As music flowed from the instrument, I noticed that the student played a simple melody while the teacher's accompaniment added depth and richness to the song. Near the end of the piece, the teacher nodded his approval.

Our life in Jesus is much more like a duet than a solo performance. Sometimes, though, I forget that He's "sitting next to me," and it's only by His power and guidance that I can "play" at all. I try to hit all the right notes on my own—to obey God in my own strength—but this usually ends up seeming fake and hollow. I try to handle problems with my limited ability, but the result is often discord with others.

My Teacher's presence makes all the difference. When I rely on Jesus to help me, I find my life is more honoring to God. I serve joyfully, love freely, and am amazed as God blesses my relationships. It's like Jesus told His first disciples, "I am the vine, you are the branches. He who abides in Me, and I in him, bears much fruit; for without Me you can do nothing" (John 15:5 NKJV).

Each day we play a duet with our good Teacher. It's His grace and power that carry the melody of our spiritual lives.

Jennifer Benson Schuldt

Abide in Me,
and I in you.

JOHN 15:4 NKJV

Write

What season caused you to lean on God more, and how did God show up for you in that time? What fruit in your life grew from drawing close to God in that season?

Connect

What word or phrase intrigues you in the excerpt below from today's passage? Take a moment to pause and allow God to share its invitation for you.

> I am the vine, you are the branches. He who abides in Me, and I in him, bears much fruit; for without Me you can do nothing. . . .
>
> As the Father loved Me, I also have loved you; abide in My love. If you keep My commandments, you will abide in My love, just as I have kept My Father's commandments and abide in His love. (John 15:5, 9–10 NKJV)

Where is God inviting you to trust Him more deeply in this season? Talk openly with God about it.

DAY 30

EZEKIEL 34:5–12

So they were scattered because there was no shepherd, and when they were scattered they became food for all the wild animals. My sheep wandered over all the mountains and on every high hill. They were scattered over the whole earth, and no one searched or looked for them.

"Therefore, you shepherds, hear the word of the LORD: As surely as I live, declares the Sovereign LORD, because my flock lacks a shepherd and so has been plundered and has become food for all the wild animals, and because my shepherds did not search for my flock but cared for themselves rather than for my flock, therefore, you shepherds, hear the word of the LORD: This is what the Sovereign LORD says: I am against the shepherds and will hold them accountable for my flock. I will remove them from tending the flock so that the shepherds can no longer feed themselves. I will rescue my flock from their mouths, and it will no longer be food for them.

"For this is what the Sovereign LORD says: I myself will search for my sheep and look after them. As a shepherd looks after his scattered flock when he is with them, so will I look after my sheep. I will rescue them from all the places where they were scattered on a day of clouds and darkness."

Jesus, the Good Shepherd, seeks out and rescues those in His care.

GOD OUR RESCUER

In the open sea, a rescuer positioned her kayak to assist panicked swimmers competing in a triathlon. "Don't grab the middle of the boat!" she called to swimmers, knowing such a move would capsize her craft. Instead, she directed weary swimmers to the bow, or front, of the kayak. There they could grab a loop, allowing the safety kayaker to help rescue them.

Whenever life or people threaten to pull us under, as believers in Jesus, we know we have a Rescuer. "For this is what the Sovereign Lord says: I myself will search for my sheep. . . . I will rescue them from all the places where they were scattered" (Ezekiel 34:11–12).

This was the prophet Ezekiel's assurance to God's people when they were in exile. Their leaders had neglected and exploited them, plundering their lives and caring "for themselves rather than for [God's] flock" (v. 8). As a result, the people "were scattered over the whole earth, and no one searched or looked for them" (v. 6).

But "I will rescue my flock," declared the Lord (v. 10), and His promise still holds.

What do we need to do? Hold fast to almighty God and His promises. "I myself will search for my sheep and look after them," He says (v. 11). That's a saving promise worth holding tightly.

Patricia Raybon

I will rescue them from all the places where they were scattered.

EZEKIEL 34:12

Write

In today's passage in Ezekiel, God identifies Himself as a good shepherd. Many of the job responsibilities of a shepherd can be found in Psalm 23—take time to jot them down. Which responsibility especially comforts you as you consider your Good Shepherd's care?

The LORD is my shepherd, I lack
    nothing.
  He makes me lie down in green
    pastures,
he leads me beside quiet waters,
  he refreshes my soul.
He guides me along the right paths
  for his name's sake.

Even though I walk
  through the darkest valley,
I will fear no evil,
  for you are with me;
your rod and your staff,
  they comfort me.

You prepare a table before me
  in the presence of my enemies.
You anoint my head with oil;
  my cup overflows.
Surely your goodness and love will
    follow me
  all the days of my life,
and I will dwell in the house of the
    LORD
  forever.

Connect

What part of today's passage grabs your attention, and why?

Pray

Choose a phrase from Psalm 23 (above), and let its words become a prayer to God, the Good Shepherd who forever watches over you.

DAY 31

1 PETER 1:6–9 NLT

So be truly glad. There is wonderful joy ahead, even though you must endure many trials for a little while. These trials will show that your faith is genuine. It is being tested as fire tests and purifies gold—though your faith is far more precious than mere gold. So when your faith remains strong through many trials, it will bring you much praise and glory and honor on the day when Jesus Christ is revealed to the whole world.

You love him even though you have never seen him. Though you do not see him now, you trust him; and you rejoice with a glorious, inexpressible joy. The reward for trusting him will be the salvation of your souls.

God knows what's best,
even when life hurts.

REFINED IN THE FIRE

Twenty-four karat gold is nearly 100 percent gold with few impurities. But that percentage is difficult to achieve. Refiners most commonly use one of two methods for the purification process. The Miller process is the quickest and least expensive, but the resulting gold is only about 99.95 percent pure. The Wohlwill process takes a little more time and costs more, but the gold produced is 99.99 percent pure.

In Bible times, refiners used fire as a gold purifier. Fire caused impurities to rise to the surface for easier removal. In his first letter to believers in Jesus throughout Asia Minor (northern Turkey), the apostle Peter used the gold-refining process as a metaphor for the way trials work in the life of a believer. At that time, many believers were being persecuted for their faith in Christ. Peter knew what that was like firsthand. But persecution, Peter explained, brings out the "genuineness of [our] faith" (1 Peter 1:7).

Perhaps you feel like you're in a refiner's fire—feeling the heat of setbacks, illness, or other challenges. But hardship is often the process by which God purifies the gold of our faith. In our pain we might beg God to quickly end the process, but He knows what's best for us, even when life hurts. Stay connected to the Savior, seeking His comfort and peace.

Linda Washington

Pray

Where might God be refining your faith in this season? Let Jesus know how it feels to be in the midst of this refinement process.

Connect

Like gold purified by fire, how has God allowed suffering to purify your heart and refine your character over the last few years?

Write

According to 1 Peter 1:6–9, how do hardship and suffering refine us as Christians? What is the reward for persevering under trial?

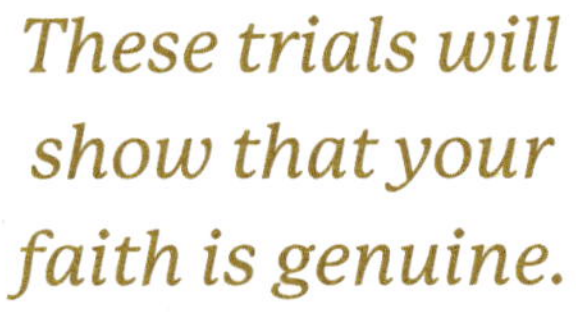

These trials will show that your faith is genuine.

1 PETER 1:7 NLT

DAY 32

EPHESIANS 2:4–10 NLT

But God is so rich in mercy, and he loved us so much, that even though we were dead because of our sins, he gave us life when he raised Christ from the dead. (It is only by God's grace that you have been saved!) For he raised us from the dead along with Christ and seated us with him in the heavenly realms because we are united with Christ Jesus. So God can point to us in all future ages as examples of the incredible wealth of his grace and kindness toward us, as shown in all he has done for us who are united with Christ Jesus.

God saved you by his grace when you believed. And you can't take credit for this; it is a gift from God. Salvation is not a reward for the good things we have done, so none of us can boast about it. For we are God's masterpiece. He has created us anew in Christ Jesus, so we can do the good things he planned for us long ago.

You're handpicked to fulfill God's good purposes.

SMALL YET MIGHTY

There are times late at night in North America's harsh Sonoran Desert where one can hear a faint, high-pitched howl. But you probably wouldn't suspect the source of the sound—the small yet mighty grasshopper mouse, howling at the moon to establish its territory.

This unique rodent (dubbed the "werewolf mouse") is also carnivorous. In fact, it preys on creatures few would dare mess with, such as the scorpion. But the werewolf mouse is uniquely equipped for that particular battle. It not only has a resistance to scorpion venom but can even convert the toxins into a painkiller!

There's something inspiring about the way this resilient little mouse seems custom-made to survive and even thrive in its harsh environment. As Paul explains in Ephesians 2:10 (NLT), that kind of marvelous craftsmanship characterizes God's designs for His people as well. Each of us is "God's masterpiece" in Jesus, uniquely equipped to contribute to His kingdom. No matter how God has gifted you, you have much to offer. As you embrace with confidence who He's made you to be, you'll be a living witness to the hope and joy of life in Him.

So as you face whatever feels most menacing in your own life, take courage. You may feel small, but through the gifting and empowerment of the Spirit, God can use you to do mighty things.

Monica La Rose

Connect

You are "God's masterpiece" (Ephesians 2:10 NLT). Take inventory of how you are uniquely created in this time and place to fulfill God's plans and purposes:

Personality traits:

Strengths, gifts, and talents:

Skills or expertise (developed through experience):

Circumstances (financial, social, educational, geographical):

Pray

Let God gently remind you of your beauty, identity, and unique purposes in His kingdom.

Write

What creatures, like the grasshopper mouse, inspire you through their resourcefulness and ability to thrive? Let your wonder point you to their Creator, and take a few minutes to praise the One who lovingly created them and you!

We are God's masterpiece. He has created us anew in Christ Jesus, so we can do the good things he planned for us long ago.

EPHESIANS 2:10 NLT

DAY 33

GENESIS 9:12–17

And God said, "This is the sign of the covenant I am making between me and you and every living creature with you, a covenant for all generations to come: I have set my rainbow in the clouds, and it will be the sign of the covenant between me and the earth. Whenever I bring clouds over the earth and the rainbow appears in the clouds, I will remember my covenant between me and you and all living creatures of every kind. Never again will the waters become a flood to destroy all life. Whenever the rainbow appears in the clouds, I will see it and remember the everlasting covenant between God and all living creatures of every kind on the earth."

So God said to Noah, "This is the sign of the covenant I have established between me and all life on the earth."

He is always present, completely faithful, and endlessly loving no matter the challenges we face.

RAINBOW HALO

On a hike in the mountains, Adrian found himself above some low-lying clouds. With the sun behind him, Adrian looked down and saw not only his shadow but also a brilliant display known as a Brocken spectre. This phenomenon resembles a rainbow halo, encircling the shadow of the person. It occurs when the sunlight reflects back off the clouds below. Adrian described it as a "magical" moment, one that delighted him immensely.

We can imagine how similarly stunning seeing the first rainbow must have been for Noah. More than just a delight to his eyes, the refracted light and resulting colors came with a promise from God. After a devastating flood, God assured Noah, and all the "living creatures" who've lived since, that "never again [would] the waters become a flood to destroy all life" (Genesis 9:15).

Our earth still experiences floods and other frightening weather that results in tragic loss, but the rainbow is a promise that God will never judge the earth again with a worldwide flood. This promise of His faithfulness can remind us that though we individually will experience personal losses and physical death on this earth—whether by disease, natural disaster, wrongdoing, or advancing age—God bolsters us with His love and presence throughout the difficulties we face. Sunlight reflecting colors through water is a reminder of His faithfulness to fill the earth with those who bear His image and reflect His glory to others.

Kirsten Holmberg

My rainbow . . .
will be the sign
of the covenant
between me
and the earth.

GENESIS 9:13

Write

As the rainbow is a symbol of God's faithfulness, places visited, events witnessed, or memories cherished can be powerful reminders of God's grace in our lives. What is a memory, experience, or place that helps to anchor you in God's love?

Connect

In Genesis 9:12–17, the rainbow is a promise of God's faithfulness. What promises have you made—to yourself, to others, and to God—throughout your lifetime?

Pray

How has God steadfastly met you and your loved ones at your point of need? Take a few moments to praise Him for His constancy and care.

DAY 34

2 TIMOTHY 1:1–5 NKJV

Paul, an apostle of Jesus Christ by the will of God, according to the promise of life which is in Christ Jesus,

To Timothy, a beloved son:

Grace, mercy, and peace from God the Father and Christ Jesus our Lord.

I thank God, whom I serve with a pure conscience, as my forefathers did, as without ceasing I remember you in my prayers night and day, greatly desiring to see you, being mindful of your tears, that I may be filled with joy, when I call to remembrance the genuine faith that is in you, which dwelt first in your grandmother Lois and your mother Eunice, and I am persuaded is in you also.

The faith alive in me can spark the faith of the next generation.

THE FROSTING OF FAITH

Hand in hand, my grandson and I skipped across the parking lot to find a special back-to-school outfit. A preschooler now, he was excited about everything, and I was determined to ignite his happiness into joy. I'd just seen a coffee mug with the inscription, "Grandmas are moms with lots of frosting." Frosting equals fun, glitter, joy! That's my job description as his grandma, right? That . . . and more.

In his second letter to his spiritual son Timothy, Paul calls out his sincere faith and then credits its lineage both to Timothy's grandmother, Lois, and his mother, Eunice (2 Timothy 1:5). These women lived out their faith in such a way that Timothy also came to believe in Jesus. Surely, Lois and Eunice loved Timothy and provided for his needs. But clearly, they did more. Paul points to the faith living in them as the source of the faith later living in Timothy.

My job as a grandmother includes the "frosting" moment of a back-to-school outfit. But even more, I'm called to the frosting moments when I share my faith: Bowing our heads over chicken nuggets. Noticing angelic cloud formations in the sky as God's works of art. Chirping along with a song about Jesus on the radio. Let's be wooed by the example of moms and grandmas like Eunice and Lois to let our faith become the frosting in life so others will want what we have.

Elisa Morgan

Is there someone in your life you can mentor or encourage in faith? Invite Jesus to share what this relationship could look like.

Connect

Take a moment to thank a spiritual mentor who has inspired and encouraged you.

Write

Take time to draw up a spiritual family tree: Who are your spiritual parents and grandparents? Your brothers and sisters? The spiritual children you've nurtured and inspired? How have you encouraged each other to draw closer to God?

I call to remembrance the genuine faith that is in you, which dwelt first in your grandmother Lois and your mother Eunice, and I am persuaded is in you also.

2 TIMOTHY 1:5 NKJV

DAY 35

JOHN 1:9–14 ESV

The true light, which gives light to everyone, was coming into the world. He was in the world, and the world was made through him, yet the world did not know him. He came to his own, and his own people did not receive him. But to all who did receive him, who believed in his name, he gave the right to become children of God, who were born, not of blood nor of the will of the flesh nor of the will of man, but of God.

And the Word became flesh and dwelt among us, and we have seen his glory, glory as of the only Son from the Father, full of grace and truth.

I am a child of the King.

A ROYAL ROLE

The closer someone in a royal family is to the throne, the more the public hears about him or her. Others are almost forgotten. The British royal family has a line of succession that includes nearly sixty people. One of them is Lord Frederick Windsor, who's forty-ninth in line for the throne. Instead of being in the limelight, he quietly goes about his life. Though he works as a financial analyst, he's not considered a "working royal"—one of the important family members who are paid for representing the family.

David's son Nathan (2 Samuel 5:14) is another royal who lived outside the limelight. Very little is known about him. But while the genealogy of Jesus in Matthew mentions his son Solomon (tracing Joseph's line, Matthew 1:6), Luke's genealogy, which many scholars believe is Mary's family line, mentions Nathan (Luke 3:31). Though Nathan didn't hold a scepter, he still had a role in God's forever kingdom.

As believers in Christ, we're also royalty. The apostle John wrote that God gave us "the right to become children of God" (John 1:12). Though we may not be in the spotlight, we're children of the King! God considers each of us important enough to represent Him here on earth and to one day reign with Him (2 Timothy 2:11–13). Like Nathan, we may not wear an earthly crown, but we still have a part to play in God's kingdom.

Linda Washington

To all who did receive him, who believed in his name, he gave the right to become children of God.

JOHN 1:12 ESV

Write

In the same way God lovingly sings over the Israelites in Zephaniah 3, He speaks words of life and love over you, His beloved child. Take time to rest in God's presence as you read Zephaniah 3, and let yourself linger on a refreshing word or phrase.

> Sing, Daughter Zion;
>   shout aloud, Israel!
> Be glad and rejoice with all your heart,
>   Daughter Jerusalem! . . .
>
> "The Lord your God is with you,
>   the Mighty Warrior who saves.
> He will take great delight in you;
>   in his love he will no longer rebuke you,
>   but will rejoice over you with singing." (Zephaniah 3:14, 17)

Connect

Take a moment to look up Jesus's genealogy (Luke 3:23–38). What about it surprises you or stands out to you?

Pray

Let Jesus's love wash over you as you pray with Zephaniah 3, printed above.

DAY 36

LUKE 6:32–38

If you love those who love you, what credit is that to you? Even sinners love those who love them. And if you do good to those who are good to you, what credit is that to you? Even sinners do that. And if you lend to those from whom you expect repayment, what credit is that to you? Even sinners lend to sinners, expecting to be repaid in full. But love your enemies, do good to them, and lend to them without expecting to get anything back. Then your reward will be great, and you will be children of the Most High, because he is kind to the ungrateful and wicked. Be merciful, just as your Father is merciful.

Do not judge, and you will not be judged. Do not condemn, and you will not be condemned. Forgive, and you will be forgiven. Give, and it will be given to you. A good measure, pressed down, shaken together and running over, will be poured into your lap. For with the measure you use, it will be measured to you.

Generosity reflects
the heart of God.

GOOD MEASURE

At a gas station one December day, Staci encountered a woman who had left home without her bank card. Stranded with her baby, she was asking passersby for help. Although unemployed at the time, Staci spent $15 to put gas in the stranger's tank. Days later, Staci came home to find a gift basket of children's toys and other presents waiting on her porch. Friends of the stranger had reciprocated Staci's kindness and converted her $15 blessing into a memorable Christmas for her family.

This heartwarming story illustrates the point Jesus made when he said, "Give, and it will be given to you. A good measure, pressed down, shaken together and running over, will be poured into your lap. For with the measure you use, it will be measured to you" (Luke 6:38).

It can be tempting to hear this and focus on what we get out of giving, but doing so would miss the point. Jesus preceded that statement with this one: "Love your enemies, do good to them, and lend to them without expecting to get anything back. Then your reward will be great, and you will be children of the Most High, because he is kind to the ungrateful and wicked" (v. 35).

We don't give to get things; we give because God delights in our generosity. Our love for others reflects His loving heart toward us.

Remi Oyedele

Connect

How might God be inviting you to show generosity—whether through your time, talents, or finances?

Pray

When has God abundantly blessed you and your loved ones? Take a moment to thank Jesus for His kindness.

Write

Is there a time you experienced the biblical principle "give, and it will be given to you" (Luke 6:38)? What was that like for you?

Give, and it will be given to you.

LUKE 6:38

DAY 37

PSALM 18:28–36, 46–49 NLT

You light a lamp for me.
The Lord, my God, lights up my darkness.
In your strength I can crush an army;
with my God I can scale any wall.

God's way is perfect.
All the Lord's promises prove true.
He is a shield for all who look to him for protection.
For who is God except the Lord?
Who but our God is a solid rock?
God arms me with strength,
and he makes my way perfect.
He makes me as surefooted as a deer,
enabling me to stand on mountain heights.
He trains my hands for battle;
he strengthens my arm to draw a bronze bow.
You have given me your shield of victory.
Your right hand supports me;
your help has made me great.
You have made a wide path for my feet
to keep them from slipping. . . .

The Lord lives! Praise to my Rock!
May the God of my salvation be exalted!
He is the God who pays back those who harm me;
he subdues the nations under me
and rescues me from my enemies.
You hold me safe beyond the reach of my enemies;
you save me from violent opponents.
For this, O Lord, I will praise you among the nations;
I will sing praises to your name.

With God's strength,
I can handle anything
that comes my way.

LIGHT IN THE DARK

A severe thunderstorm passed through our new town, leaving high humidity and dark skies in its wake. I took our dog, Callie, for an evening stroll. The mounting challenges of my family's cross-country move grew heavier on my mind. Frustrated by the countless ways things had strayed so far from our high hopes and expectations, I slowed to let Callie sniff the grass. I listened to the creek that runs beside our house. Tiny lights flashed on and off while hovering over the patches of wildflowers climbing up the creek's bank. Fireflies.

The Lord wrapped me in peace as I watched the blinking lights cutting through the darkness. I thought of the psalmist David singing, "You light a lamp for me. The Lord, my God, lights up my darkness" (Psalm 18:28 NLT). Proclaiming that God turns his darkness into light, David demonstrated confident faith in the Lord's provision and protection (vv. 29–30). With God's strength, he could handle anything that came his way (vv. 32–35). Trusting the living Lord to be with him through all circumstances, David promised to praise Him among the nations and sing the praises of His name (vv. 36–49).

Whether we're enduring the unpredictable storms in life or enjoying the stillness after the rains have passed, the peace of God's constant presence lights our way through the darkness. Our living God will always be our strength, our refuge, our sustainer, and our deliverer.

Xochitl Dixon

You light a lamp for me. The Lord, my God, lights up my darkness.

PSALM 18:28 NLT

Write

What season are you in—one of storms or stillness? Whatever your season, how has God showed up for you, and been with you, in it?

Connect

Is there a word or phrase that captures your attention from Psalm 18, today's Bible passage? Linger there.

Pray

What does your heart need in this season? Invite Jesus to meet you there.

DAY 38

PSALM 8:3–4; REVELATION 21:22–25

When I consider your heavens,
  the work of your fingers,
the moon and the stars,
  which you have set in place,
what is mankind that you are mindful of them,
  human beings that you care for them? . . .

I did not see a temple in the city, because the Lord God Almighty and the Lamb are its temple. The city does not need the sun or the moon to shine on it, for the glory of God gives it light, and the Lamb is its lamp. The nations will walk by its light, and the kings of the earth will bring their splendor into it. On no day will its gates ever be shut, for there will be no night there.

When I look up and see the beauty and complexity of the universe, I remember just how amazingly creative our God is.

LOOK UP

When filmmaker Wylie Overstreet showed strangers a live picture of the moon as seen through his powerful telescope, they were stunned at the up-close view, reacting with whispers and awe. To see such a glorious sight, Overstreet explained, "fills us with a sense of wonder that there's something much bigger than ourselves."

The psalmist David also marveled at God's heavenly light. "When I consider your heavens, the work of your fingers, the moon and the stars, which you have set in place, what is mankind that you are mindful of them, human beings that you care for them?" (Psalm 8:3–4).

David's humbling question puts our awe in perspective when we learn that, after God creates His new heaven and earth, we'll no longer need the moon or the sun. Instead, said John the apostle, God's shimmering glory will provide all necessary light. "The city does not need the sun or the moon to shine on it, for the glory of God gives it light, and the Lamb is its lamp. . . . There will be no night there" (Revelation 21:23–25).

What an amazing thought! Yet we can experience His heavenly light now simply by seeking Christ, the Light of the world. In Overstreet's view, "We should look up more often." As we do, may we see God.

Patricia Raybon

As you go about your day, look up (and around). Take time to notice and feel gratitude for God's daily gifts.

Connect

Take a moment to marvel at God's creativity by filling in the blanks of Psalm 8 below and making the psalm your own:

> When I consider [identify a part of creation that inspires you
>
> ____],
>
> the work of your fingers,
>
> the [identify a part of creation that inspires you
>
> ____],
>
> which you have set in place,
>
> what is mankind that you are mindful of them,
> human beings that you care for them? (Psalm 8:3–4)

When have you been filled with a sense of wonder "that there's something much bigger than ourselves"? What was that experience like for you?

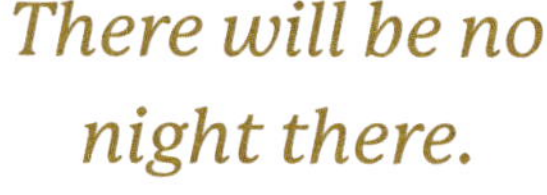

There will be no night there.

REVELATION 21:25

DAY 39

COLOSSIANS 3:1–4 NKJV

If then you were raised with Christ, seek those things which are above, where Christ is, sitting at the right hand of God. Set your mind on things above, not on things on the earth. For you died, and your life is hidden with Christ in God. When Christ who is our life appears, then you also will appear with Him in glory.

As I look "up," my spirit attunes to God's activity and purposes.

THINGS ABOVE

The cockeyed squid lives in the ocean's "twilight zone" where sunlight barely filters through the deep waters. The squid's nickname is a reference to its two extremely different eyes: the left eye develops over time to become considerably larger than the right—almost twice as big. Scientists studying the mollusk have deduced that the squid uses its right eye, the smaller one, to look down into the darker depths. The larger left eye gazes upward, toward the sunlight.

The squid is an unlikely depiction of what it means to live in our present world and also in the future certainty we await as people who "were raised with Christ" (Colossians 3:1 NKJV). In Paul's letter to the Colossians, he insists we ought to "set [our] mind[s] on things above" because our lives are "hidden with Christ in God" (vv. 2–3 NKJV).

As earth dwellers awaiting our lives in heaven, we keep an eye trained on what's happening around us in our present reality. But just as the squid's left eye develops over time into one that's larger and more sensitive to what's happening overhead, we, too, can grow in our awareness of the ways God works in the spiritual realm. We may not have yet fully grasped what it means to be alive in Jesus, but as we look "up," our eyes will begin to see it more and more.

Kirsten Holmberg

Set your mind on things above, not on things on the earth.

COLOSSIANS 3:2 NKJV

Write

Today, how may God be inviting you to "set your mind on things above" (Colossians 3:2 NKJV)?

Connect

Prayerfully read Colossians 3 and allow yourself to linger on a word or phrase that captures your attention. Why might it be meaningful at this moment?

> If then you were raised with Christ, seek those things which are above, where Christ is, sitting at the right hand of God. Set your mind on things above, not on things on the earth. For you died, and your life is hidden with Christ in God. When Christ who is our life appears, then you also will appear with Him in glory. (vv. 1–4 NKJV)

Where are you struggling to look up today? Let Jesus help you. He cares about you!

DAY 40

MARK 14:3–9

While he was in Bethany, reclining at the table in the home of Simon the Leper, a woman came with an alabaster jar of very expensive perfume, made of pure nard. She broke the jar and poured the perfume on his head.

Some of those present were saying indignantly to one another, "Why this waste of perfume? It could have been sold for more than a year's wages and the money given to the poor." And they rebuked her harshly.

"Leave her alone," said Jesus. "Why are you bothering her? She has done a beautiful thing to me. The poor you will always have with you, and you can help them any time you want. But you will not always have me. She did what she could. She poured perfume on my body beforehand to prepare for my burial. Truly I tell you, wherever the gospel is preached throughout the world, what she has done will also be told, in memory of her."

Ordinary actions motivated by love have everlasting significance.

SHE DID WHAT SHE COULD

She loaded the plastic container of cupcakes onto the conveyor belt, sending it toward the cashier. Next came the birthday card and various bags of chips. Hair escaped from her ponytail, crowning her fatigued forehead. Her toddler clamored for attention. The clerk announced the total and the mom's face fell. "Oh, I guess I'll have to put something back. But these are for her party," she sighed, glancing regretfully at her child.

Standing behind her in line, another customer recognized such pain. Jesus's words to Mary of Bethany echoed in her mind: "She did what she could" (Mark 14:8). After anointing Him with a bottle of expensive nard before His death and burial, Mary was ridiculed by the disciples. Jesus corrected His followers by celebrating what she had done. He didn't say, "She did all she could," but rather, "She did what she could." The lavish cost of the perfume wasn't His point. It was Mary's investment of her love in action that mattered. A relationship with Jesus results in a response.

In that moment, before the mom could object, the second customer leaned forward and inserted her credit card into the reader, paying for the purchase. It wasn't a large expense, and she had extra funds that month. But to that mom, it was everything. A gesture of pure love poured out in her moment of need.

Elisa Morgan

Connect

Who would you like to interview from today's story (Mark 14:3–9)? Take a few moments and have a "conversation" with him or her. What do you learn from the conversation? Does anything surprise you?

Pray

As you wrap up, what would you like God to know? Take a few minutes to have an honest conversation with Jesus and to thank Him for how He's shown up for you over the past forty days.

Write

In the last forty days, how has God revealed His love to you in new, fresh ways? How has Jesus drawn close to you?

She did what she could. She poured perfume on my body beforehand to prepare for my burial.

MARK 14:8

CONTRIBUTORS

To read more from these writers, visit odbm.org/devotionals.

Anne Cetas

Poh Fang Chia

Xochitl Dixon

Kirsten Holmberg

Cindy Hess Kasper

Alyson Kieda

Monica La Rose

Elisa Morgan

Ruth O'Reilly-Smith

Remi Oyedele

Patricia Raybon

Lisa M. Samra

Jennifer Benson Schuldt

Linda Washington

Anna Haggard, General Editor, is associate content editor for Our Daily Bread Publishing. A follower of Jesus, she loves to write and edit books sharing about God's generous, deep love for all people. Anna coauthored the Called and Courageous Girls series, and she lives in Lancaster, Pennsylvania.

Seek and she will find

Spread the Word by Doing One Thing.

- Give a copy of this book as a gift.
- Share the QR code link via your social media.
- Write a review of this book on your blog, favorite bookseller's website, or at ourdailybreadpublishing.org.
- Recommend this book to your church, small group, or book club.

Connect with us.

Our Daily Bread Publishing
PO Box 3566, Grand Rapids, MI 49501, USA
Email: books@odbm.org

Connect with us.

Our Daily Bread Publishing
PO Box 3566, Grand Rapids, MI 49501, USA
Email: books@odbm.org